THE MERCHANT OF VENICE

Teacher's Guide

Copyright © 1988 Harcourt Brace Jovanovich Canada Inc.
55 Horner Avenue, Toronto, Ontario
M8Z 4X6

Canadian Cataloguing in Publication Data

Roy, Ken.
  The merchant of Venice. Teacher's guide

(HBJ Shakespeare)
Supplement to: Shakespeare, William, 1564-1616.
The merchant of Venice.
Includes text of the play.
Bibliography: p. T25
ISBN 0-7747-1292-9

1. Shakespeare, William, 1564-1616. The merchant of Venice.
I. Law, Harriet, 1931-   . II. Maitman, Mark.
III. Waldron, Ian.   IV. Shakespeare, William, 1564-1616.
The merchant of Venice.   V. Title.   VI. Series.

PR2825.R69 1988   822.3′3   C88-094130-8

Printed in Canada

88 89 90 91 92 5 4 3 2

HBJ SHAKESPEARE

THE MERCHANT OF VENICE

Teacher's Guide

Series Editor: Ken Roy
Contributing Author: Harriet Law
Notes for The Merchant of Venice: Mark Maitman, Ian Waldron

Harcourt Brace Jovanovich, Canada

Toronto   Orlando   San Diego   London   Sydney

Table of Contents

Shakespeare's England

Approaches to *HBJ Shakespeare's The Merchant of Venice*

An Introduction to *HBJ Shakespeare*

PHILOSOPHY OF *HBJ SHAKESPEARE*

HBJ Shakespeare was developed in response to a growing need for an integrated language arts and student-centred approach to the study of Shakespeare. By providing a wide range of writing, speaking/listening, viewing, and independent project activities that allow for personal and creative response, this series assists students to recognize both the accessibility of Shakespeare's plays and the relevance of the plays to their own experience, and gives them the opportunity to explore Shakespeare in ways meaningful to them.

Students are encouraged to become familiar with and involved in the plays from the beginning of their reading by using these features common to all *HBJ Shakespeare* editions.

TEXT FEATURES

- Getting started – provides students with activities related to important themes in the play for discussion and/or written response.

- In this scene – gives students a brief scene description, allowing them to anticipate the issues they will encounter in the scene.

- For the next scene – offers students one or two predictive questions that draw upon their experience and provides them with a bridge to the next scene.

- Text notes – provide students with explanations for Shakespeare's text and help eliminate difficulties students may have with the language. These notes appear on pages that are facing the Shakespeare text and are aligned with the line(s) of text they explain.

- Illustrations – contribute detailed and historically accurate visual representations of characters and events. Illustrations appear at the beginning of each act and at the beginning of most scenes and help the students enter the world of the play.

- Activities — provide for personal writing, speaking, reading, viewing, and independent project responses from students at the end of scenes, or groups of scenes, and at the end of the play.

THE ACTIVITIES

The activities encourage students to further explore the issues they considered before and during their reading of the scenes. These interpretive and creative activities appear after all major scenes, after groupings of minor scenes, and at the end of acts. Activities that consider the whole text appear at the end of the play. Many of the activities are recommended for group work. (All the benefits of group work — such as accepting responsibility for learning, using expressive and receptive modes of communication in brainstorming, problem solving, and establishing a shared goal — can be derived as well from the study of Shakespeare as they can from any other area of study.) In selecting and completing individual activities, students discover opportunities to:

- discuss the play, drawing upon their own experience;
- discuss and/or write about their feelings and responses to characters, situations, and concepts;
- make generalizations they can apply to new situations;
- complete independent learning projects;
- keep personal journals;
- create directors' logs;
- improvise, role play, or dramatize scene segments;
- make video recordings.

The activities at the end of the play are generally intended to synthesize students' experiences of the play as a whole. Many of these activities will require more time to complete than the end-of-scene activities.

Note: It is not expected that students should complete all activities at the end of a scene or complete activities for all scenes. Students and/or teachers should select activities appropriate to the students' interests and abilities.

HBJ Shakespeare allows students to join in the learning process by becoming actively involved in the play. We hope teachers and students will share in this dynamic experience of Shakespeare with both a feeling of comfort and a sense of confidence.

AN OVERVIEW OF THE TEACHER GUIDE

Section II of this guide offers strategies for presenting *HBJ Shakespeare* and for presenting a play in a condensed time period (approximately three to five weeks).

Section III offers historical and interpretive information about Shakespeare's England.

Section IV offers ideas for presenting *The Merchant of Venice* and includes

- a rationale for teaching the play,
- specific classroom activities and strategies,
- additional activities related to the issue of prejudice,
- suggestions for presenting *The Merchant of Venice* in a condensed time period,
- a selection of classroom resources.

HBJ Shakespeare Activities

THE ACTIVITIES

The activities following scenes and acts call on students to use inferential, analytical, interpretive, and creative skills in their responses. Students should always be clear about the teacher's expectations for completing these tasks meaningfully. Note that, because activities vary in scope and require varying lengths of time to complete, students will need assistance in selecting activities, and time provided for them to share or present their responses.

No one grouping of activities in an *HBJ Shakespeare* play will fit all class situations. It is extremely important, therefore, for the teacher to plan ahead, know the abilities and interests of the class, and have clearly stated objectives for the presentation of the scenes, acts, and activities to be undertaken.

Because many of the activities at the end of acts require more than the assignment portion of class time to complete, students should have the opportunity to work on them as the class study of the scenes progresses.

Care should be taken not to overload students with activity tasks. It is important to remember that although some students have developed skills in directing their own learning and are able to select and complete activities, others will need practice and support in developing these skills.

An overview of activities found in *HBJ Shakespeare* and strategies for facilitating student response to them follows.

Writing

The writing activities present opportunities for students to write in a variety of modes and genres, for different purposes, and to different audiences. These activities include writing items such as news articles, press releases, psychological reports, interviews, letters, journals, and editorials. To integrate a full writing program (including pre-writing, revising, and publishing activities) with the study of Shakespeare in a limited amount of time, you might choose a sequence of procedures such as the following:

Pre-writing
Pre-writing is often an on-going activity in which the student rehearses ideas for possible inclusion in writing assignments. The product of pre-writing could be a journal entry or notes made to prepare for a particular type of writing.

Students reading *Hamlet* might, for example, write a news report issued by the Palace Corps about Claudius's decision to send Hamlet to England. As a pre-writing activity they may wish to make notes about structures and styles of news reporting they observed when comparing the same news event written in several different newspapers.

Revising
Revising can occur at any time during the writing process. If students wish to have peer feedback before revising writing assignments, they could arrange peer group conferences. As a student reads his/her writing in progress, and points out a difficulty, other members of the group could offer ideas that may have worked for them in resolving a similar problem.

Publishing
Before students publish their written material, they may wish to apply a checklist including items such as points of grammar, punctuation, and syntax to their work. Students could publish a casebook or newspaper about the play, containing their writings during/at the end of the study of the play. They may prefer to put their news reports on the bulletin board following the revision stage.

Journal Activities
Students may wish to keep journals – a personal record of responses to issues in the text. Sometimes, these entries will be private reflections. Many entries, however, will be ones that students would enjoy sharing with a peer, in a group, with the teacher, or with the whole class. Teachers lend authenticity and demonstrate a commitment to writing by using the class writing time to create their own journal writing entries as writing models. These entries could also be shared.

Independent Learning Project Activities
Independent learning project activities provide students with the opportunity to direct their own learning as they explore new areas

of study or develop skills to complete tasks they set for themselves. Many students show considerable aptitude for completing independent research and learning assignments while others may need practice and support in developing the necessary skills for acquiring knowledge independently.

The following is an example of an independent activity. It is from the Act 1, Scene 1 Activities for *Romeo and Juliet*.

There are references to the mythological god and goddess Cupid and Diana in this scene. Find out as much as you can about each of these characters. What significance do they have for Romeo in this scene? Why have mythological characters such as Cupid and Diana remained so popular to readers, viewers, and writers, to the present day?

As you do research, discuss your work with the teacher to make sure you are on the right track. Keep all your notes and rough drafts in a folder.

Present a summary of your findings in an essay, a chart, or an audio-visual form at the end of the time specified for this independent activity.

The completed assignments may be presented to the teacher/class independently or in a group presentation such as a debate, a seminar, or a video presentation.

Scene Rehearsal Activities
These activities allow students to develop their dramatic perceptions of the play as they consider motivations for speeches and ways of choreographing actions, and requirements for settings and props.

When students consider the physical dimensions of an action, they often find that the dramatic content becomes clearer in their minds. For example, students often have difficulty following the sequential movement and seating arrangements in the banquet scene in *Macbeth*; but when they choreograph the scene, they gain a clearer sense of what happens and are better able to understand the cause of Macbeth's hallucinations. Likewise, when students act out the confusing word-games between Launcelot and his father in Act 2, Scene 2, of *The Merchant of Venice*, they appreciate more fully the humour and comic interplay in the scene.

Students could rehearse scene segments in small groups. While students are acting, you could move from group to group observing and highlighting problems they are experiencing rather than offering solutions. When students raise questions about their problems in interpreting lines dramatically, you could ask, "Why is that a problem for you?" You might ask questions such as "Would the character be standing or sitting when he/she says the lines?" "Why do you think so?" Then look for a group that has prepared an interesting interpretation of a scene segment and have them present it to the class.

Director's Log

A director's log is a recording, either in note form or tape, of the ideas the group's scene-rehearsal leader wishes to keep for reference.

After a group rehearsing a scene segment chooses its director, he/she becomes responsible for conducting the group through problems it may have interpreting scene speeches and actions.

The director's log is the official record of decisions the group has reached with regard to the interpretations and the staging of the scene segment. It might include information such as

- how the group will create the scene segment,
- how the group will choreograph the action,
- where the group will place the action,
- what predominant mood the group will create for the action.

The log might also include the group's differences of opinion related to speeches, actions, and staging.

The log could record, as well, events that precede and follow the scene segment to give it context.

Directors who tape discussion related to scene-segment interpretations often find that their group gains helpful insights to the dynamics of idea-sharing by listening to the taped discussions.

The director's log activity is a useful strategy for having students combine some or all of the following skills: speaking, listening, writing, and problem-solving.

Improvisation

Students often like to speculate about different characters' behaviour. By improvising, students often understand the behaviour of these characters better. It is easier for students to improvise a scene segment than it is for them to write a summary of the scene. When students improvise, they gain a sense of the character's motivation. Directors often use improvisation as a way of warming up actors for their roles. In improvisation activities, students use their imagination and their personal experiences to transform characters' speeches and so enlarge the life of the characters in their minds.

Listening

Recordings

Recordings of selected scenes or specific speeches can be used to spark discussion about characters' motives and feelings.

Music

Students might enjoy choosing and taping music they feel would appropriately accompany a particular scene. A student (or group) preparing a reading of the scene could choose the music; or you could have one student (or group) prepare a reading while another prepares the "theme" music.

Viewing

Film

To provide students with a sense of the whole play, you might set aside two or three periods for this viewing activity. Watching a film of the play allows students to:

- acquire a sense of the plot, character relations, and shape of the play in one experience;
- appreciate the historical aspect of the play by seeing the costumes;
- gain a sense of the setting;
- become familiar with the language; and
- see the integration of language with character and actions.

Make a Video

This activity is time-consuming and requires careful planning and close monitoring. The time needed, from script to show-time, is approximately three weeks. Even the camera-shy student can become involved in the activity in some capacity. This activity stresses process as much as product and while it is a video activity, it is also a writing-process activity: it teaches concepts about narrative construction; characterization; setting, theme, and symbols; point of view; and the importance of proofreading, editing, and revising. Perhaps most important, it teaches co-operation and team work.

Presenting *HBJ Shakespeare* in a Condensed Time Period

Some teachers may need to present the Shakespeare play in a condensed time period (approximately three to five weeks). The following suggestions offer ways to present the play using the student-centred approach in this series.

SINGLE FOCUS APPROACH

The class could preview part or all of the play by viewing a film to establish a focus for experiencing the play, such as one of the following:

- a central character,
- a central theme,
- a central image pattern.

Having chosen one of the above as their primary focus in reading the text, students could then select to complete the activities related to that focus.

Central character, theme, image, focus

Shakespeare characters who are vital and inherent parts of the play experience and whose behaviour profoundly affects the plot development are appropriate choices for understanding and responding to the whole play through the single character focus.

In *Julius Caesar*, for example, it is Brutus (whom we first encounter in Act 1, Scene 2), whose behaviour most significantly brings the plot to its climax and denouement. The main themes of the play are revealed in his decisions and actions. Through Brutus, the personal and political conflicts of the play are resolved. Brutus, then, is a vital character in this play.

After choosing Brutus as their single character focus for *Julius Caesar*, students could direct their attention to parts of important scenes that include Brutus. Scenes such as the ones in the first two acts that introduce students to Brutus's strengths and weaknesses, to the important decisions he makes, and to the assassination scene; the funeral scene; the final farewell between Brutus and Cassius; and Brutus's death might be considered. Students could then complete activities which focus on Brutus to further explore the language of the play, the relationships between Brutus and others, and his character.

Macbeth is a play which is particularly suitable for emphasizing the single theme focus: power corrupts. *Hamlet* lends itself to the analysis of the central image pattern of decay and disease as a way of understanding both the characters and the themes.

In using the single focus approach, students have an opportunity to observe and respond to the play in depth within the condensed time allottment.

STORY-TELLING AND/OR VIDEO APPROACH

To provide students with a complete learning experience of a Shakespearean play, it is not necessary to have them use a detailed or in-depth reading approach to all scenes. Students often respond enthusiastically to the vibrancy of the dramatic experience when the play is brought to life by a story-telling or video presentation. After establishing the focus and direction of the play through reading with students the initial scenes, you (or selected students) could present subsequent scenes using an animated story-telling approach. This technique encourages students to discover meanings they may not find by reading the lines of text. Similarly when students view scenes, they often gain a srtonger sense of the drama than they do by following the lines on paper. Students who respond critically, not only to a script, but to the choices made by actors, directors, and designers, are well on their way to becoming enthusiastic and discriminating theatre-goers.

In *The Merchant of Venice*, the scenes in which Morocco and Arragon make their casket choices are particularly effective when viewed without prior preparation by the class. The costumes, sets, facial expressions, and accents of the performers bring to life scenes which students might otherwise find uninspiring. *The Merchant of Venice* also provides excellent opportunities for story-telling as a means of rapid study. The entire sequence of events from the receipt of Antonio's letter in Belmont (Act 3, Scene 2) to the beginning of the trial (Act 4, Scene 1) could be conveyed by an animated teacher report or a series of student reports.

KEY SCENES APPROACH

After you and your students have previewed the play to decide what aspect (characters, theme, plot-line) is of most interest, you might designate segments of the play for attention. Below is a suggested procedure for approaching the five acts in a condensed time period.

One-third of the time for Act 1

Act 1 should be given careful attention so that characters and their motivations are clearly established, the issues and themes are made clear, and the plot is clarified. You may prefer to do this by playing a recording, by showing a video or movie version of the act, by using rehearsed readings, or by group discussions. Whatever method you choose, it should be one with which the students feel comfortable.

A focussed study of the first act of the play is important. It gives students the opportunity to identify characters and their motives, themes, and essential conflicts. Once they have familiarized themselves with the first act, students will feel more comfortable completing the activities throughout the rest of the play.

One-third of the time for Acts 2 and 3

Select important plot development and/or character interaction scenes to use as springboards for class discussion and involvement in end-of-act/scene activities related to key issues. Since it is impossible to have students explore all the play's conflicts and themes, assist students in determining topics they may choose to develop in their activity response.

Students could make journal entry responses to scenes from Acts 2 and 3 that are not focussed during class time.

One-third of the time for Acts 4 and 5

Focus on key scenes from Acts 4 and 5. The last scene of Act 5 should include discussion about the major conflicts, issues, and themes in the play, recalling discussions about them in Act 1, so that students experience a sense of completion.

A final writing, dramatic, or viewing activity could result from this discussion. The group might wish to have a "video day" viewing of the ending of a film or video version of the play. They could choose to have a discussion about the play as comedy/tragedy (history) or to present a dramatization of selected segments of student-prepared scenes. Students might wish to debate major issues in the play.

Summing up is important because it leaves the play complete in students' minds and, although not all the issues will have been covered, students will have achieved their own experience of Shakespeare.

See Suggested Strategies for Teaching *The Merchant of Venice* in a Condensed Time Period, page T43.

Shakespeare's England

HBJ Shakespeare encourages students to bring their experiences to the play. Like Shakespeare's audiences, students know about love, loyalty, taboos, leadership, revenge, identity, and ambition. As Shakespeare wrote in a time very distant and different from our own, however, students will likely better appreciate the plays if they have some context for Shakespeare's world. You might wish to use the historical information that follows as your own resource and discuss these topics with students during their study of the play. A bibliography for Shakespeare's England appears on page T25.

WHO WAS WILLIAM SHAKESPEARE?

During Shakespeare's lifetime (1564–1616), England was ruled by Elizabeth I (1558–1603) and James I (1603–1625). Because Shakespeare was a commoner and only the nobility kept formal chronicles of themselves, we have only a few facts about his life. He was baptized on April 26, 1564, at Stratford-upon-Avon. Since it was customary to baptize on the third day, we can assume he was born on April 23. We know that he was the third of John Shakespeare's and Mary Arden's eight children and that his father was a glovemaker, a grain-dealer, and a man of some importance in the town who served as alderman and mayor.

Shakespeare attended a grammar school in Stratford-upon-Avon where the chief emphasis (as in all such schools) was on Latin. How long he remained there is not certain, but in 1583, at the age of eighteen, he married Anne Hathaway. Her home, in the adjacent village of Shottery, is now known as Anne Hathaway's cottage and has long been a main tourist attraction for Stratford visitors. The couple had three children: Susannah, born in 1583, and twins, Hamnet and Judith, born in 1585. Susannah married and had a child, Elizabeth, who also married but had no children. Hamnet died in 1596, at the age of eleven. Judith married, but her children did not live. In three short generations, the direct lineage of Shakespeare died out.

Sometime between 1585 and 1591, Shakespeare moved to London where we assume he spent most of his adult life. How he became an actor and a playwright we don't know, but we do know that he became one of the chief stockholders in the most important theatre company of the time (the Lord Chamberlain's Men) and a part owner of the Globe theatre. We also know that he became famous enough to draw a scathing insult from another playwright, an envious one perhaps, named Robert Greene, who called him "an upstart crow, beautified with our feathers."

When the Lord Chamberlain's Men were taken under the patronage of King James I, their name was changed to the King's Men. In this company were some of London's best actors, including Richard Burbage and Will Kempe. Shakespeare both wrote and acted for this company.

In London, Shakespeare made enough money to buy a coat of arms, giving himself the official status of "gentleman." For unknown reasons, he returned to Stratford-upon-Avon in 1612 to live in one of its finest houses, New Place. He lived there until he died, at age fifty-two, on the date of his birth.

The exact dates for Shakespeare's plays are not known. The following list gives a general frame of reference:

COMEDIES	TRAGEDIES	HISTORIES
1591		Henry VI, Part I
1592 The Comedy of Errors		Henry VI, Part II
1592 Two Gentlemen of Verona		Henry VI, Part III
1593 Love's Labour's Lost	Titus Andronicus	Richard III
1594		King John
1595 A Midsummer Night's Dream	Romeo and Juliet	Richard II
1596 The Merchant of Venice		
1596 Taming of the Shrew		
1597		Henry IV, Part I
1598 Much Ado About Nothing		Henry IV, Part II
1599 As You Like It	Julius Caesar	
1599 The Merry Wives of Windsor		Henry V
1601 Twelfth Night	Hamlet	
1602 Troilus and Cressida		
1602 All's Well That Ends Well		
1604 Measure for Measure	Othello	
1605	King Lear	
1606	Macbeth	
1607	Timon of Athens	
1607	Antony and Cleopatra	
1608 Pericles		
1609	Coriolanus	
1610 Cymbeline		
1611 The Winter's Tale		
1611 The Tempest		
1613		Henry VIII

WHAT WAS LONDON LIKE IN SHAKESPEARE'S TIME?

London in the 1590s was a bustling city of about 200,000 people. One of the first things that Shakespeare might have noticed was the great number of churches in the city. London was known as the city of churches.

The city was still walled as it had been for many years, but it was growing rapidly. People flocked to the city, causing a building boom of staggering proportions. The streets were narrow, cobblestoned in places, but always dirty and crowded. Sanitation was unknown and plagues were common.

Shakespeare lived first in St. Helen's parish near Bishopgate Street and later near Cripplegate and across the river in Southwark. It was an exciting city for a young man from the country – full of strange sights and sounds. Since it was the age of exploration, there were many exotic sights such as clothing from the Arab countries, masks and charms from Africa, goods from China, and strange fruits and vegetables such as the tomato and the potato.

Since London was a port city, many languages were heard in the streets, such as French, Italian, Dutch, and Russian. A popular pastime was learning to speak these new languages, particularly French. Londoners received their education by reading books which spread in profusion with the advent of the printing press. It is estimated that there were over fifty printing presses in operation in London during this time. There were no public libraries or newspapers but "broadsides" (one page sheets printed on both sides) that reported news happenings in the community – especially murders, fires, deaths of important people, disasters of all kinds and, occasionally, bits of history – were sold for half a penny all over London on almost all street corners.

The streets were crammed with humanity. People begged for food and cried out for alms, shopkeepers called out to passersby to purchase their wares, balladeers sang on street corners, church bells called citizens to prayer, coaches clacked over the cobblestones, and water-bearers staggered under their loads. Londoners worked a twelve-hour day.

In addition to the noisy, sprawling markets, there were shops everywhere imaginable. Clothing was sold on London Bridge. Goldsmiths, grocers, fishmongers, and ironmongers also staked out areas to sell their wares. Even the wall around London itself gave way to shops.

Londoners loved entertainment and much of it was free. There were water games on the Thames, a small zoo in the Tower of London, cock-fights, bear-baitings, public executions, and, of course, plays, including those of Shakespeare himself, that covered just about any subject a Londoner might be interested in.

Despite the roughness of the period, it was not necessarily an unkind environment. Londoners gave generously to the poor, and London merchants experimented with various methods of finding work for the poor and the unemployed. And there was Queen Elizabeth, who made frequent appearances to the delight of the citizens.

Permanent theatres were rapidly replacing the old inn-yards as places of entertainment, and great actors were emerging to form acting troupes. New playwrights were springing up to supply the theatres with new plays. Shakespeare arrived in London when the theatres were thriving. It was a wonderful and glorious time in which to be alive and working in one of the most vibrant cities in the world.

WHAT WERE THE THEATRES FOR SHAKESPEARE'S PLAYS LIKE?

Inn-yards were favourite places for play performances in Elizabethan England because they provided a ready-made audience and because their long, narrow entrances and surrounding balconies served as makeshift theatres.

Stages were probably improvised from any available materials – some must have been quite precarious. The inn's stables and outbuildings likely would have served as change rooms, and stage properties would have been at a minimum. In the early years of these productions, performers took up a collection at the end of each play. In later years, the performers contracted with the yard-keeper to have him charge admission.

As plays grew in popularity, some actors considered having a permanent facility for their work. James Burbage, a popular actor admired by Shakespeare, built one of the first permanent theatres in 1576. To pacify the Puritans, who believed that plays were sinful, Burbage built his playhouse, called the Theatre, outside the city walls in Shoreditch. In 1577, another theatre, the Curtain, was also built in Shoreditch. The problem with Shoreditch, however, was that patrons had to walk over fields and swamps to get there. For this reason, theatre builders later chose Bankside, an area across the river from the still theatre-prohibiting city, in what is now called Southwark. In 1587 the Rose was built in Southwark, and in 1595, the Swan was erected there.

When Richard, son of James Burbage, ran into difficulties with his landlord over renewing the lease for the land on which his father's playhouse stood, he decided to move. He entered into an agreement with five of his fellow actors, one of them being Shakespeare, to build a new theatre called the Globe on Bankside in 1599. The Globe had an octagonal shape with a "thrust" stage projecting into the body of the theatre so that an audience surrounded the actors on three sides. There were three levels of balconies which enclosed the stage and an open pit in the middle that accommodated the poorer patrons. Drawings of the Globe indicate that only the balconies and some of the pit and stage were covered by a thatch roof. The rest of the theatre was exposed to the elements.

The Globe's stage was primitive by our standards. It had doors on both sides for entrances and exits and a recessed area which could serve as an inner stage. There was little room for storage or props and elaborate scenery. Above the stage recess was a balcony, and the floor had a trap door. The stage could be used, therefore, to represent heaven, earth, and hell — symbolism that would have been readily understood by an Elizabethan audience.

The Elizabethan stage provided an intimacy between actor and audience not possible in modern curtained theatres. This intimacy was sometimes hazardous for the actor if the audience were unhappy with the performance. (Some audiences, disappointed with the performances, became quite violent.) Theatrical innovations, such as the soliloquy and other devices to indicate the speedy passage of time typical of Elizabethan theatre, worked well on this simple stage.

The last big Elizabethan theatre, built in 1600, and called the Fortune, was square, unlike the O-shaped theatres that had been the norm. A stage similar to the Fortune's square stage was built in Stratford, Ontario, in the Festival Theatre, during the 1960s. Today we can see plays written by Shakespeare presented in much the same way as they had been presented for the audiences of his time.

As quickly as they sprang up, the Elizabethan theatres with their thrust stages died out, in part because they were licensed to make money for the owners, who traded on a popular interest of the time, much as rock concert promoters do today. Elizabethan theatres fulfilled a need, and when that need died, so did the theatres.

The Actors
Since all Elizabethan actors were male, all female roles were played by boys or men. It was not easy for the actors to appear convincing in female roles in broad daylight to their highly critical Elizabethan audiences. Actors were also required to perform very stylized and difficult dances that often needed both superior acrobatic skills and exceptional physical stamina. The dancing requirements were likely easy in comparison with the fight scene requirements, however.

Actors were expected to fight as expert swordsmen. They needed technical skills and training as well as excellent physical conditioning to recreate duels and/or battle scenes without injuring themselves or their opponents. They had to perform actions such as running a sword through another actor's head or tearing out his entrails without impairing the opponent's usefulness for the next day's performance. Audiences of the day expected to see bloody deaths and mutilations in fight scenes. When bloodshed was involved, actors used sheep's blood because it had the right consistency for "running" well and it provided the audience with "real" blood. In stabbing scenes, actors wore concealed bladders of blood under their costumes. These bladders could be ruptured by retractable knife blades. When this action was performed correctly, the bladder worn by the character being stabbed was punctured, the blood spewed forth in profusion, and the audience cheered with glee. Performed badly, the actor being stabbed was injured (not an infrequent occurrence) and had to be carted off the stage, probably also to cheers from the audience. In this case another actor had to fill in. Since acting companies were small (perhaps twelve or fifteen men), actors were required to play many parts convincingly, often on short notice, and always to a demanding audience. Acting was a hazardous occupation in Elizabethan England!

The Audience

They were a rough group of people, usually consisting of working-men, trade apprentices from London, seamen on leave, and country visitors to the city in search of cheap entertainment. They were frequently noisy, boisterous, and given to violent outbursts of disapproval if their expectations were not met. They loved the sound effects, including cannons, drums, and chilling screams; the extravagant costumes; and the props, such as guillotines, fountains, and ladders. Most of these people stood on the ground, and so acquired their name, "groundlings." Dramatists like Shakespeare disliked these lower-class individuals and often portrayed them as humorously foolish and unsuccessful imitators of the educated people in their plays.

Surrounding the theatre were vendors, prostitutes, con-men, and pickpockets. Some patrons with money sat on benches in the balconies, while those who wanted to display their finery could rent stools on the stage. Members of the nobility may have attended the theatre for sheer adventure, but they usually arranged to have plays performed in their own homes.

The growing middle class attended a different type of theatre, which was indoors, had artificial lighting, special effects, a sophisticated satirical style, well-trained boy actors, and a higher entrance fee. Shakespeare's company of actors eventually purchased one of these "private" theatres (The Blackfriars), and produced many of his later plays there.

In an age in which the printing press widened literacy but could not possibly affect the lifestyle of the many illiterates, the theatre offered both a ready source of information and good entertainment.

WHAT WAS IT LIKE TO LIVE IN SHAKESPEARE'S TIME?

Shakespeare grew up in the Renaissance, a chaotic period of history. It was marked by both the vigour of powerful changes and the aftermath of drastic political upheavals. The decline of feudalism gave new importance to what would eventually become a rising middle class of merchants, shopkeepers, and professionals.

There was a sense of enthusiasm for expansion encouraged by Queen Elizabeth's emphasis on trade and travel to increase the nation's wealth. There were new ideas coming from students and teachers at the universities, and a sense of vitality in London that added to the energy and excitement.

During the Renaissance in England, guidance in spiritual matters was transferred from the Pope to the monarch, establishing the importance of individual conscience. Reformers began to look to education and the study of the classic works of Greece and Rome as alternatives to a single authority for matters of spiritual guidance.

On one hand, there were feelings of vitality, optimism, and national pride during the reign of Elizabeth. On the other hand, there was financial strain resulting from the prolonged trade wars with Spain. Toward the end of Elizabeth's reign there was also an increasing anxiety resulting from her having no heir apparent, a circumstance that would later plunge the nation into a disastrous civil war over the succession.

Shakespeare's life (1564–1616) straddled this period of hopeful change and the disillusionment that resulted from the corrupt reign of James I. Plays Shakespeare wrote during James I's reign include tragedies such as *Macbeth, Othello*, and *King Lear*.

WHAT WERE PEOPLE'S BELIEFS?

Not all people shared the same moral beliefs. Mercy, sin, pride, repentance, moderation, kingship, and God's power, however, were all central issues – important topics for sermons, for private conscience, and for literary exploration. The dramatic interest in Shakespeare's plays usually centres on the ways in which characters resolve spiritual, ethical, and political choices involving these issues. In both *Romeo and Juliet* and *The Merchant of Venice*, the issue of mercy is approached through a blending of Christian and classical ethics. In these and many other plays, Shakespeare portrayed the integration and balance of moral qualities as the basis of virtue and sound action.

"Providence," "fortune," and "chance" were important concepts to the Elizabethan people. Those who believed in Providence thought that God provided for and took care of those who trusted in Him. Protestants felt that Providence intervened directly when the winds changed in England's favour during the attempted invasion by the Spanish Armada. The evidence of providence was called fortune, a concept related to a person's fate. The image of fortune was often represented by a wheel upon which a person's career rose or fell.

Events manipulated by fortune were called "chance." Chance implies a sense of the randomness of life's incidents, which undermines any security we might have in predicting cause and effect. In *Hamlet*, we see Hamlet balance his desire for revenge with his concern that he may be misinterpreting providential "signs." In *Macbeth*, we see Macbeth realize that there are both good and evil implications in "chance": it may crown him King, but it may also expose his guilt when guardian angels "blow the horrid deed in every eye." In *The Merchant of Venice*, we see chance disguised in many forms: in the business risks Antonio takes as a matter of course; in the casket test; in Bassanio's readiness to risk all to afford the opportunity to woo Portia; in the agreement Antonio makes with Shylock. The comedic resolutions of the play represent, in many ways, a safe passage through the hazards of chance.

Of special importance to *The Merchant of Venice* is the attitude of Shakespeare's contemporaries to foreigners. Despite the cosmopolitan flavour brought to London by its port, the English outlook remained insular. For the most part, people mistrusted foreigners, with their strange customs, habits of dress and languages. Attitudes towards continental Europeans, Jews, Moslems, even Scots, were largely informed by cultural stereotypes which presented foreigners either as figures of ridicule or as a threat. Shakespeare may ultimately transcend stereotypes in his characterization, but he frequently begins with foreigners drawn precisely as his audience would expect to see them. It is important that modern students see Shakespeare's stereotyping in this context so that they may have the opportunity to judge for themselves whether the playright's humanity extends beyond the boundaries of his own place and time.

BIBLIOGRAPHY FOR SHAKESPEARE'S ENGLAND

The following references may be helpful to teachers and students if historical reading is desired.

Baugh, Albert C., Editor. *A Literary History of England*. Appleton-Century-Crofts, 1948

Bindoff, S.T. *Tudor England*. Penguin Books, 1969

Bowers, Fredson. *Elizabethan Revenge Tragedy*. Princeton University Press, 1966

Ferguson, Margaret F. *Rewriting the Renaissance*. University of Chicago Press, 1986

Frye, Roland Muskat. *Shakespeare and Christian Doctrine*. Princeton, University Press, 1963

Harrison, G.B. *Introducing Shakespeare*. Penguin Books, 1966

Holman, C. Hugh. *A Handbook to Literature*. Bobbs-Merrill Educational Publications, 1977

Joseph, B.L. *Shakespeare's Eden: The Commonwealth of England 1558–1629*, Blanford Press, 1971

Sandler, Robert, *Northrop Frye on Shakespeare*. Fitzhenry and Whiteside, 1986

Tillyard, Eustace M. *The Elizabethan World Picture*. Random House, 1959

Wilson, J. Dover. *Life in Shakespeare's England*. Cambridge University Press, 1962.

Approaches to *HBJ Shakespeare*
The Merchant of Venice

THE PLAY AND THE TEXT: A RATIONALE

Why teach *The Merchant of Venice*?

A great Jewish teacher, known to history as Jesus Christ, said that the Old Testament, the Bible of the Jews, depends upon two central commandments:

> Thou shalt love the Lord thy God with all thy heart . . . ,
> and
> Thou shalt love thy neighbour as thyself.
> *(Matthew* 22: 37–39)

This latter love, called charity by St. Paul, is held to be the primary moral tenet of Christianity: it leads to understanding, common humanity and peace between people and between nations.

Unfortunately, following this principle is not as easy as it sounds. Pride, fear of the unknown, and suspicion of strangers are all human emotions which make it difficult for us to accept and trust those whose beliefs, or culture, or colour, are different from our own. And yet, no matter what our religion, or whether we believe in a god at all, our ethical conscience tells us that it is right to struggle against these emotions, to strive to love our neighbour and be charitable to all people, even to those who appear to be enemies.

The Merchant of Venice is a play about the triumph of charity, written in a time when charity was thought to be a particularly Christian virtue. It is, therefore, like all of Shakespeare's comedies, a triumph of Christianity – that is, of the moral principle upon which Christianity is based.

It is evident, however, that the characters in this play, whether they be called Christians or Jews, display a remarkable lack of charity throughout most of the story. This should not surprise us. In order for there to be a triumph, there must be a conflict; if charity (love) is to win out, it must win out over its opposite – hatred. Antonio (the Christian) hates Shylock (the Jew) as much as Shylock hates Antonio, and this hatred leads both of them to the brink of disaster. (This near disaster is an *essential* part of comedy, according to Northrop Frye.)

Surrounding this central conflict, however, is the bigotry and prejudice of an entire society, which, though calling itself Christian, has forgotten the message of Christ himself – the message of charity. Shylock's *reason* for wanting to get rid of Antonio is "strictly business": the Christian, by defamation of Shylock and by lending money *gratis*, was severely hampering Shylock's business. But the Jew, no simple villain, would never have acted as he did on this reason alone: he needed a *motive*, something to impel him towards murder. This is what the elopement plot provides. Shylock is disgraced, robbed, and ridiculed by the Christian community of Venice. He feels justified in taking a full measure of revenge.

The movement of the play, then, is towards a tragedy of hatred, like *Romeo and Juliet*. Shylock is given several chances to prevent a tragedy, but for him it is too late. His hatred, a product of resentment, pain, and anger, has grown too strong: even an angel of charity cannot move him. But Antonio is still salvageable. Brought to the point of death himself by Shylock's hatred, he appreciates the divine message of charity – and saves his enemy.

It is easy to understand why some people have called the play anti-Semitic: the Jew is vanquished; Christianity triumphs. And it is true that Christianity triumphs – but not over Judaism. Shylock does not act according to any Jewish principles but, as he admits in the play (Act 3, scene 1, lines 49–69), according to the corrupt model provided by the so-called Christians of Venice. This "fallen" type of Christianity, then, is vanquished by the spirit of true Christianity, which, as Jesus observed, is also the spirit of Judaism. Thus, the Jew who had been the victim of a corrupt and fallen Christianity becomes the beneficiary of a faith renewed.

In preparing a new edition of the play for secondary schools, we have been keenly aware of the objections which have been voiced over its use as a school text. To recommend using *The Merchant of Venice* in the classroom is not to pretend that the issue of cultural stereotyping does not present a problem. We *are* concerned about the plight of the "minority" student in the classroom and outside it, and we take seriously the obligation of all teachers to encourage tolerance and understanding in their students. Our response to this challenge springs from two beliefs. First, we believe that a person's early teenage years are the *right* time to introduce questions about hatred, bigotry, and stereotyping, and that the classroom is the right place – a controlled environment, where prejudices can be examined and critized, where irrational responses can be exposed to the light of reason. Second, we think that this play, when presented sensitively, provides an outstanding opportunity for students to encounter these important issues for themselves: to learn about the pervasiveness – and the dangers – of cultural stereotyping, to see the effects of bigotry on the human personality (both of the victim and of the agent), to reflect upon how many of history's wars and tragedies have stemmed from the intolerance of difference, and to recognize the common humanity that unites us as ultimately greater than the differences that divide us. This edition of *The Merchant of Venice*, then, is committed to the position that when students are given the opportunity to understand the background, the issues, and the characters – *all* the characters – by bringing *their own* experience to bear upon the play, they will find the study of the play to provide a significant step in their own enlightenment.

Why use a student-centred approach?
Experience is the best teacher.

There are two ways in which the adage applies to the study of a Shakespeare play. First, it is the core of Shakespeare's universality that his plays appeal to the minds and hearts of all people at all times: what this really means is that we have all had experiences which make his plays meaningful for us. *So have our students.* Though they are not familiar with medieval Venice or Elizabethan England, they know about friendship, family loyalty, persecution, and the desire for revenge. In suggesting a "student-centred" approach to Shakespeare, we are simply saying that the students' *own* resources are to be used in teaching the play; that they be asked to bring their own experience to the work, to see analogies to their own world, to think about patterns in human behaviour, to become actively involved in exploration and discovery, rather than to remain passive receivers of information. The paedagogical rationale for this approach is well documented (Piaget, Dewey, Whitehead) and has recently been reinforced by new discoveries about ways the brain functions (Rico, Parnes, DeBono, Edwards). But, for the classroom teacher, the most convincing argument is what our own experience tells us: that when students are actively involved in learning, they enjoy it more; and when they enjoy it, they care about it; and when they care, their learning is deeper and more lasting.

The second application of the adage arises from Whitehead's observation, in *The Aims of Education,* that education should not be preparation for a "life" to begin once school is over – the student's life is going on right now. If schooling is devoid of real experience, it is hollow and fruitless. And "real" experience is defined by what the students themselves *do*. In this text, students are invited to experience Shakespeare through a variety of *activities* which demand not only that they think using both hemispheres of the brain, but that they *act* on their thinking.

CLASSROOM ACTIVITIES AND STRATEGIES

Introducing the text

If this is your students' first experience with Shakespeare, or their first experience with a student-centred approach to literature, you might wish to assist them in becoming comfortable with the text by allowing time to discover the discuss features of its organization, design, and format. Begin with "To the Reader," the letter which appears at the beginning of the text and introduces students to the response-based approach they will encounter as they work through it. Allow students to flip ahead to find examples of each textual feature: *For the next scene* . . . , "In this scene . . . ," textual notes, illustrations, end-of-scene activities. Distinguish between the textual apparatus and the actual text of the play itself, stressing the obvious fact that Shakespeare's script is to provide the focus of attention.

You could also develop, with the students, a list of objectives for studying the play. A typical class list might include some of the following objectives:

- To acquire and develop an understanding and enjoyment of the play.
- To practise both independent and group skills as a way of bringing meaning to the text of a play.
- To use personal experiences and perceptions to enlarge the meanings of the play.
- To investigate how the written script can be interpreted dramatically.
- To use writing as a way of refining feelings about the play.
- To use creative imagination as a way of bringing new meaning to the play.
- To record how language is used effectively to enhance themes, reveal character, and convey attitudes.
- To note how our language is a changing language.

Whether or not students become actively engaged in the design of objectives, teachers themselves must begin with a clear understanding of why they have chosen this particular text, how they plan to use it as a vehicle for learning, and what they hope to accomplish with students through the study of the play.

"Getting Started" provides an introduction to the specific issues and concerns of *The Merchant of Venice*. This section is worth at least a class reading before students begin their study of the play, for it does focus their attention on the themes Shakespeare explores and it does establish the relevance of the play to their own experience. Taking time to explore the issues raised in this introductory activity – either in small group discussion or in journals – is particularly important for students who might be intimidated by the text of the play itself or for students who do not instinctively seek active engagement with a literary text. Your use of the questions in *Getting Started* may also set out an approach for introducing individual scenes. The questions in "For the next scene . . ." sections similarly focus attention on the contemporary relevance of central concerns in each scene or group of scenes.

Even if you wish to move as quickly as possible to the text of the play, point out the *Dramatis Personae*. You may want to return to this list when new characters are introduced, in order to establish relationships between them. You could also use the *Dramatis Personae* to comment briefly upon the social hierarchies at work within medieval Venice and Elizabethan England.

A Word of Caution!
The potential for controversy in *The Merchant of Venice* may tempt some teachers to introduce the play too carefully or to justify it to excess before students have had a chance to respond to it themselves. We suggest you resist this temptation. The student-centred approach is founded on the primacy of exploration, discovery, and response by the student. An introduction that biases that process (such as the reading of the selection in this teacher's guide on "Why Teach *The Merchant of Venice*") may well jeopardize the spontaneity and authenticity of students' responses to the play: students who know what it is they are "supposed" to find in the play may simply go through the motions of discovery.

Experiencing the play
Studying the Scenes
What follows is one approach to the use of this text with a class. It is offered here as a suggestion, not as a formula to which all classes should rigidly adhere.

Pre-reading (*"For the next scene"*)
The questions in these sections are intended to stimulate thought about the issues in the upcoming scene. Depending on time con-

straints, students may respond through personal journal writing, in small group exchanges, or in a directed whole class discussion. Teachers should encourage sincerity rather than looking for "correct" responses, and should try to direct the students into a *dialogue with each other* as opposed to a question and answer session with the teacher.

In this scene
The scene synopsis might be read by the class together. This would be a good time to invite students to comment upon the illustration at the start of every scene. They could consider its depiction of setting, costume and character.

Reading the scene
Although these comments apply directly to reading the scene, we suggest you encourage variety in the way students encounter the play, by allowing them to view or listen to parts of it (see page T 00).

If students are reading the scene aloud, insist on lively voice characterizations, and lead by example. A good reading alone can unlock much of the mystery of Shakespeare. Use the facing page notes to solve small problems as they arise. Ensure that vocabulary, syntax and plot are under control, and take note of significant advances in character and thematic development. Help students make connections with the discussion that preceded the reading.

First response
If time permits, you may wish to have students record their immediate responses to a scene in a short personal journal entry before going on to the activities.

Choosing activities
Your own objectives for the class will determine the selection of some activities; the students themselves should be allowed to pursue others according to *their* own interests. Try to build flexibility into the work period: individuals, pairs and groups can profitably work at a variety of tasks at the same time, as long as all students have a clear idea of what they have to do, the time in which they have to do it, and the requirements for presentation of their findings (see also "Sharing and De-briefing")

Doing the activities: the teacher's role
At this stage, the teacher should act as a facilitator and a resource, promoting participation and a full experience of the play. Circulate among students, whether they are working alone or together:
• remind them to refer to the text to account for their ideas and support their opinions.

T31

- encourage precise speaking and courteous but critical listening.
- provide feedback when it is invited.
- when needed, re-direct discussions toward their goals and objectives.
- direct students to other resources that may assist them.

Sharing and debriefing
Every activity session should lead to some form of sharing of results. Students should know in advance whether this sharing will be formal or informal, oral or written, and whether they will be asked to present their conclusions to individuals, groups or the whole class. You should also consider short de-briefing sessions after the assignments have been completed, especially at the early stages of group work. The class should discuss how well they did the work, what problems they had, and why they had those problems. The aim of the debriefing is to improve group productivity for subsequent assignments.

Whatever your approach to the use of the resources in the text, students should always be certain about your expectations. When students know what is required of them, they are able to respond to activities with increased commitment and achievement. As students become familiar with the student-centred approach to reading, understanding, and enjoying Shakespeare, they will be able to engage themselves in the learning experience with little teacher direction or interference. The teacher can then assume the role of guide and resource. No matter how readily students adapt to the approach of the text, teachers should take note of the warnings on page T9.

Using the activities
As we have already outlined, HBJ Shakespeare activities draw on a wide spectrum of thinking, reading, writing, speaking, listening, and creative skills. This section of the guide suggests some ways in which you might approach individual questions and assignments.

1. Exploration of the script as drama
Shakespeare's plays were never intended to be read. As scripts, they were meant to be seen and heard. Many of the activities in this text invite students to explore and experiment with the possibilities of the play as a theatrical event. A commitment to the integrity of the theatre experience and the power of the spoken word is evident in the first activity in the student book (Act 1, Scene 1 Activities, page 18). We consider this to be an important assignment for both those students who have and those who have not studied Shake-

speare before. The exercise allows students to embody the language with character and personality. If possible, allow students to make an audio or video tape of their efforts. In this way, they will be able to discuss and evaluate their experiments and to shape final presentations without the pressure of live performance. Similarily, professional recordings and videotapes of the play will provide students with the opportunity to compare and assess different versions of a speech or scene.

Additional activities of this type:

Act 1	Scene 3	Activity 2	(Shylock's first aside)
Act 2	Scene 2	Activity 1	(expansion of a soliloquy)
Act 2	Scene 2	Activity 2	(dialogue played for humour)
Act 3	Scene 1	Activity 3	(developing the role of Tubal)
Act 3	Scene 4	Activity 1	(experimenting with Portia)
Act 5	Scene 1	Activity 2	(finding wit in the lovers' dialogue)

Another group of theatre-related activities requires students to explore the script from the perspectives of the director. One general suggestion for using director's log activities has already been presented (page T14). There are, however, other approaches that you might prefer for specific activities in this text. The first activity for Act 2, Scene 1, asks students to investigate the scene as an opportunity for spectacle and pageantry on the stage. It leads students to explore costume, sound, set, and choreography as a means of achieving impact on an audience. The instructions for this particular question suggest individual notes in a director's logbook. It is a valuable exercise for students to compare their notes with those of other "directors" in the class. An equally productive approach is to begin work in small groups. Students can experiment, improvise, and brainstorm the possibilities of the scene together, before recording their ideas and decisions in individual logs.

Additional activities of this type:

Act 2	Scenes 3–6	Activity 3	(casting Launcelot)
Act 3	Scene 2	Activity 1	(the creation of suspense)
Act 3	Scene 2	Activity 3(c)	(the use of music)
Act 3	Scene 3	Activity 2	(inclusion/exclusion of a scene)
Act 4	Scenes 1–2	Activity 8	(conveying an interpretation)
Act 5	Scene 1	Activity 2	(musical selections for the play)

Because each of these activities has been designed primarily to encourage the full exploration, discussion, and appreciation of Shakespeare's script as drama, any of them could be used for classroom performance or for making an audio or video recording.

Activities that ask students to assume the persona of Shakespeare himself also focus on the script as drama. Students have to justify the playwright's inclusion of specific speeches, scenes, and sequences. They are drawn, in this way, to examine the play as a unified dramatic whole. Activity 4, following Act 2, scene 9, requires students to explore Shakespeare's reasons for including the scene in which the Prince of Arragon makes his choice of the silver casket. Since the audience already knows that Portia's portrait is contained within the leaden casket, the students must argue that the scene fulfills some other significant function within the play as a whole.

Additional activities of this type:

Act 3	Scene 2	Activity 3(b)	(Shakespeare defends his hero and heroine)
Act 4	Scene 1–2	Activity 12	(Shakespeare explains the purposes of the ring plot)
Act 5	Scene 1	Activity 5(b)	(Shakespeare writes a sequel to the play)

2. Contemporary and Personal Parallels

In addition to the pre-reading questions which appear in "For the next scene . . . ," a significant number of post-scene activities require students to discover and investigate parallels between the text and their own lives. The ability to personalize and contemporize the issues of the play helps students to understand more completely both the world of the play and the world in which they live. At the end of the opening scene, there are several questions which introduce students to this process of active interrelationship with the text. Activity 2 asks students to explore the imagery of the opening lines of the play and to create a list of contemporary images suitable for a play about a modern business person. Activities 3 and 6 ask students to investigate their own relationships with friends in order to understand the relationships among the characters in this scene. Activity 3 asks students to consider the roles they play in their daily lives and to compare their roles with the role Gratiano describes.

Additonal activities of this type:

Act 1	Scene 2	Activity 1	(advice from a modern Nerissa)
Act 1	Scene 2	Activity 3	(confiding in a friend)
Act 1	Scene 3	Activity 4	(money-lending as banking)
Act 1	Scene 3	Activity 5	(Shylock's predicament)

Act 2	Scene 2	Activity 4	(modern comedians/Launcelot and Gratiano)
Act 3	Scene 3	Activity 3	(rewriting of a scene)
Act 4	Scene 1	Activity 6	(situation ethics)
Act 4	Scene 1–2	Activity 9(b)	(the fairness of Shylock's sentence)
Act 4	Scene 1–2	Activity 10	(courtroom conventions)
Consider the Whole Play		Activity 3	(identifying with Shylock)

3. Predictions

One of the skills that the student-centred approach develops is the ability to "think into" a work, to allow expectations to be moulded by the experience of each scene, yet to be changed as events develop. For the student who can read this way, each scene becomes another piece of the puzzle, to be fitted into the context which has already been developed and understood.

One way of developing this skill is to encourage students to predict what will happen next at various stages. These predictions must not be capricious or arbitrary, but should be grounded in the context established by the present scene. For example, activity 6 following Act 1, scene 2, asks students to think about the obstacles in the way of Portia and Bassanio's eventual marriage. Students should have recognized that there are two: Bassanio's poverty and the casket lottery. Asking students how these obstacles might be overcome allows them to fit Shakespeare's plot into their own pattern of thinking.

Additional activities of this type:

Act 1	Scene 3	Activity 7	(the foreshadowing of future events)
Act 2	Scene 3–6	Activity 1	(the elopement as a complicating factor in the loan plot)
Act 2	Scene 9	Activity 3	(predicting Bassanio's choice of casket)
Act 3	Scenes 4–5	Activity 2	(predicting Portia's plan)
Act 5	Scene 1	Activity 5(b)	(sequel to the play)
Consider the Whole Play		Activity 7(c)	(reinventing plot outcome)

In addition, worthwhile exercises in predictive thinking might come out of class discussion or the students' own questions about the play.

4. Language Study Activities

Any study of Shakespeare is, by definition, the study of language. The plays are a treasure house of metaphor, allusion, image, pun, wit, irony, rhetoric, dynamic word choice, and colourful expression. As students explore the characters, conflicts, and themes of the play, they become increasingly familiar with its poetry and language, gradually acquiring the ability to understand a scene on first hearing and to appreciate Shakespeare's language as communication rather than an obstacle to meaning.

Language-related activities in this text focus student attention on the uses of language to create character, establish conflict, and explore theme.

Additional activities of this type:

Act 1	Scene 1	Activities 4 + 5	(examination of language to reveal character)
Act 1	Scene 2	Activity 3	(exploration of language to reveal relationship)
Act 1	Scene 3	Activity 2	(exploration of aside to reveal character)
Act 1	Scene 3	Activity 4	(paraphrase)
Act 2	Scene 2	Activity 3	(malapropism)
Act 4	Scenes 1–2	Activity 4	(epitaphs)
Act 4	Scenes 1–2	Activity 5	(analysis of Portia's speech)

In addition, the textual notes serve as language study aids. Without deflecting student attention from the experience of the play itself, we have tried to design the notes as opportunities for student discovery about language rather than as aids to "translating" a foreign text. Students should be encouraged to expand their own working vocabularies as they encounter new and useful words in the text. They should also be encouraged to collect and commit to memory short passages of the play which they find particularly appealing.

5. Creative Exploration

Even reluctant students welcome an opportunity to extend their imaginations beyond the text in order to create the "missing" letters, speeches, dialogues, and scenes which do not appear in the play. Moreover, when learning is achieved through such a process of exploration and discovery, it is often thorough. Many of the activities in this book invite students to use their imaginations to enter into a personal relationship with the play. They write letters in the roles of various characters: as a modern Nerissa, for example, giving advice to Portia (Act 1, Scene 2, Activity 1), or as Portia's father, explaining to his daughter the rationale of the casket lottery (Act 1, Scene 2, Activity 2). They also write as characters Shakespeare did not invent, like the detective Shylock might have hired to investigate the disappearance of his daughter (Act 2, scenes 3–6, Activity 5).

Act 1	Scene 3	Activity 6(b)	(lawyer's reaction to the bond)
Act 2	Scene 8	Activity 3	(Jessica's letter to Shylock)
Act 3	Scene 1	Activity 4	(Shylock's letter to Leah)
Act 3	Scene 2	Activity 7	(Duke's request for advice)
Act 4	Scenes 1–2	Activity 4	(writing epitaphs)
Act 5	Scene 1	Activity 4	(explanation of how Antonio's ships were saved)

Some of the creative exploration exercises require *dramatic* products, either scripted or improvised. For example, students are invited to create the scene in which Shylock sends Tubal to search for his missing daughter (Act 3, Scene 1, Activity 2), or to act out the "conspiracy" between Portia and Nerissa before Bassanio's choice is made (Act 3, Scene 2, Activity 3(a)).

Additional activities of this type:

Act 1	Scene 2	Activity 5	(Portia's interview with a suitor)
Act 2	Scene 8	Activity 4(b)	(dialogue between Antonio and Bassanio)
Act 2	Scene 9	Activity 2	(dialogue between Morocco and Arragon)

Still other exercises require a combination of analytical and creative thinking skills. After their first encounter with the Prince of Morocco, for example, students are asked to interview him, as if for a newspaper or television (Act 2, Scene 1, Activity 2). The same approach is taken to Portia and Antonio after the courtroom victory in Venice (Act 4, Scenes 1–2, Activity 11). Again, after the famous courtroom scene, students are asked to analyze the legality of procedures in the case, and then to recreate the scene taking these legal issues into account (Act 4, Scene 1, Activity 10). These creative exercises generate enthusiasm and deepen understanding, especially if students are encouraged to share the products with each other.

6. Media-Related Activities

This text emphasizes the experience of the play as theatre. Nonetheless, there are a variety of activities which encourage writing and taping for other media and investigate parallels between the play and the students' own experience of contemporary television and film:

Act 1	Scene 2	Activity 1	(newspaper advice column)
Act 2	Scene 1	Activity 2	(radio or television interview)
Act 2	Scene 7	Activity 2	(biased reporting)
Act 2	Scene 8	Activity 4	(soap opera/melodrama)
Act 4	Scene 1	Activity 11(c)	(interviews for a feature article)
Consider the Whole Play		Activity 4	(publication of a newspaper)

We think it is essential to use recordings and films as part of the student experience of the play. If resources are available, you should also consider making of a video as a profitable and appropriate activity for selected groups of students.

7. Debates

Formal debating allows students to explore important issues in the play while developing critical thinking and fluent speaking style. It provides a way of discussing controversial issues rationally rather than emotionally, and ensures that the students consider the validity of opposing points of view. We recommend that students approach a debate resolution by generating arguments on *both sides* of the issue before they know which side they will be supporting.

Classroom debates usually follow a parliamentary model, requiring two two-member teams and a speaker. The format of the debate is quite straightforward:

The Prime Minister supports the resolution (5 minutes maximum).
The first opposition member speaks (including a rebuttal) (5 minutes maximum).
The second government member speaks (5 minutes maximum).
The Leader of the Opposition speaks (7 minutes maximum).
The Prime Minister concludes (2 minutes maximum).

Some important rules of parliamentary debate should be established:

Points of Order: A debater may rise on a point of order during an opponent's speech in order to point out a breach of procedure. Common points are irrelevance to the resolution, unparliamentary language, and failure to address the Speaker. After the point has been stated, the Speaker of the House must rule upon it by stating that the point *is* or *is not* well taken.

Points of Personal Privilege: Members may rise if they feel that they have been misquoted or grossly misrepresented by an opponent. Again, the Speaker will make a ruling, which is final.

Use of Notes: In debating, the ability to think and speak *ex tempore* is all-important. Debaters could use point-form notes, but no debater should be allowed to read a prepared text.

Rebuttal: The skill of listening is central to good debating. Emphasize the importance of responding directly to what opposing speakers have said, and pointing out the weaknesses in opponents' arguments.

We suggest that debates *not* be assigned to a whole class, but that different groups within the class be assigned different topics. In this way, several debates might be presented during the study of the play.

Debating Activities:

Act 1	Scene 3	Activity 8	(Bassanio's character)
Act 2	Scenes 3–6	Activity 5	(Shylock as father)
Act 3	Scene 2	Activity 5	(Portia's speech on marriage)
Act 4	Scenes 1–2	Activity 7	(Bassanio's behaviour in the courtroom)
Consider the Whole Play		Activity 2	(seven topics)

8. *Journal Writing*

There are times during the study of this play when students must be given the opportunity to respond with complete freedom, without concern for how anyone else might react to their thoughts. This is especially true where a sensitive issue, such as personal prejudice, is involved.

At these moments in the play, it has been our practice to suggest *personal journal* responses, either as a first step toward formulating an opinion for public airing, or simply to clarify a position for oneself.

In the earlier activities, students are simply asked to think about controversial or complex issues by imagining themselves in similar situations. Activity 5 in Act 1, Scene 3 is this type: here students must try to apply some of Shylock's problems to their own lives. The results should remain personal and confidential.

In some cases, you could ask students to go on from journal writing to discussion. For example, students could compare their reactions to Solanio's famous speech ridiculing Shylock's misery (Act 2, scene 8, activity 1). Remember, however, that these activities should be handled with care. You may feel that your students are not yet ready to discuss the issues honestly and without inhibition. If so, it would be better to take the activity no further than journal writing.

In other cases, we have suggested that a discussion might conclude with a journal entry. An example is activity 4, following Act 3, scene 2. In such cases, we think that the final stage of reflection should remain personal.

Additional activities of this type:

Act 1	Scene 2	Activity 4(c)(d)	(response to Portia's prejudice)
Act 3	Scenes 4–5	Activity 2	(predicting Portia's actions)
Act 4	Scenes 1–2	Activity 1	(explaining Shylock's behaviour in court)
Act 4	Scenes 1–2	Activity 5(a)	(interpreting Portia's speech on mercy)
Consider the Whole Play		Activity 1	(seven suggested topics)
Consider the Whole Play		Activity 3	(identifying with Shylock)

9. Partner and Small Group Work

The pair and group activities in this text are designed with a range of communication skills in mind: idea generation (brainstorming), critical thinking and listening, organization, and evaluation. The simplest partner and group activities (such as Act 1, scene 1, activity 1; and Act 3, scene 3, activity 3) demand only cooperation and the uncritical sharing of ideas. It is important that students begin co-operative learning with this kind of non-threatening exercise, before moving on to ones that require a critical comparison of ideas (such as Act 1, scene 3, activity 8). In an atmosphere of non-competitive sharing, students may attempt the more complex problems, especially those which require the achievement of a consensus (Act 2, scenes 3-6, activity 2) or those which entail the sharing of emotional responses (Act 3, scene 2, activity 4).

Additional activities of this type:

Act 1	Scene 1	Activity 6	(improvising/scripting)
Act 1	Scene 2	Activity 5	(scripting an interview)
Act 1	Scene 3	Activity 2	(rehearsing a speech)
Act 1	Scene 3	Activity 4	(evaluating speech composition)
Act 2	Scene 1	Activity 2	(improvising an interview)
Act 2	Scene 1	Activity 3	(discussing Portia's behaviour)
Act 2	Scene 2	Activity 1	(expanding a soliloquy)
Act 2	Scene 2	Activity 4	(analyzing humour)
Act 2	Scenes 3–6	Activity 7	(discussing Jessica's actions)
Act 2	Scene 7	Activity 1	(relating costume and set to theme)
Act 2	Scene 8	Activity 4	(improvising/scripting)
Act 2	Scene 9	Activity 1	(comparing Arragon and Morocco)
Act 2	Scene 9	Activity 2	(improvising/scripting)

10. Critical Thinking

Several activities in this text require students to catalogue, organize, interpret, and/or evaluate textual information. Students are asked to draw inferences, to make judgements, to compare, to clarify, and to speculate about developing characters and events.

For example, after Act 1, scene 1, activity 4 asks students to reach some specific decisions about Bassanio's personality, motives, and values. Later questions about Bassanio will invite the students to review and re-assess these first impressions as they work toward a final interpretation of his character. Similar sets of activities are applied to the characters of Antonio and Shylock.

Additional activities of this type:

Act 1	Scene 2	Activity 6	(clarifying Portia's response to Bassanio)
Act 1	Scene 2	Activity 4(c)	(questioning Portia's prejudice)
Act 2	Scenes 3–6	Activity 6	(considering Jessica's elopement)
Act 2	Scene 8	Activity 1	(examining Solanio's cruel humour)
Act 2	Scene 9	Activity 3	(predicting an outcome)
Act 3	Scene 1	Activity 1	(analyzing Shylock's speech on revenge)
Act 3	Scene 1	Activity 3	(analyzing Tubal's role)
Act 3	Scene 2	Activity 2	(sharing observations)
Act 3	Scene 2	Activity 6	(charting relationship of plots)
Act 3	Scene 2	Activity 3	(interpreting clues in the final casket scene)
Act 3	Scenes 4–5	Activity 1	(reading/interpreting/evaluating)
Act 3	Scenes 4–5	Activity 3	(analyzing subtle scene differences)
Act 4	Scenes 1–2	Activity 1	(analyzing Shylock's behaviour in court)
Act 4	Scenes 1–2	Activity 5	(interpreting Portia's speech on mercy)
Act 4	Scenes 1–2	Activity 6	(weighing ethical arguments)
Act 4	Scenes 1–2	Activity 10	(analyzing travesties of conventional courtroom procedure)
Act 4	Scenes 1–2	Activity 9(b)	(assessing Shylock's sentence)
Act 4	Scenes 1–2	Activity 11	(preparing media interviews)
Act 5	Scene 1	Activity 2	(choosing music)

Act 5   Scene 1   Activity 4   (evaluating final outcome)
Consider the Whole   Activity 7(c) (reinventing a plot)
Play

11. Research and Independent Learning

Several of the activities included in the "Consider the Whole Play" section give students opportunities to pursue their interests and investigations beyond the play itself. These activities are intended to develop those skills in organization, library research, note-taking, interviewing, and especially self-discipline which are essential to success in higher education.

For these activities, teachers should be prepared to help students narrow their focus and decide upon the precise nature of their product. If students are to avoid frustration, they need a good deal of direction. The format, length, and thesis of an independent project might be decided on between student and teacher and formalized in an independent study contract.

Additional Activities for Dealing with the Issue of Prejudice

You may wish to study *The Merchant of Venice* without treating the issue of prejudice in depth. However, you might find that students themselves turn their attention to this source of controversy. The following activities should allow you to direct their investigations to constructive understanding and conclusions.

1. As you already know, Shakespeare began his creation of the character of Shylock with a stereotype. Although there were no Jews in England in Elizabethan times, the stereotype was alive in the current literature and superstition of Shakespeare's countrymen.
   Research the stereotype of the medieval Jew, particularly in European literature. Your focus should not be on an accumulation of characteristics and examples, but on an understanding of *why* this stereotype developed.

   Some useful sourcebooks include:
   Anti-Semitism: A Concise World History (James Parkes)
   The Jew in the Medieval World: A Source Book (J. Marcus)

   Do not forget that a good encyclopedia should provide an excellent beginning to your research.
   Present your findings in an essay or class report.
2. Research the history of Shylock on the stage. Use one of the books listed below to discover how great actors of the past have influenced the way we see this character today:

Shylock on the Stage (Toby Lelyveld)
Shylock: The History of a Character (Hermann Sinsheimer)
The Truth about Shylock (Bernard Grebanier)

In a small group, rehearse *one scene* as it would have been played by two of the following in the role of Shylock: Edwin Booth, David Garrick, Henry Irving, Edmund Kean, Charles Macklin, or Laurence Olivier. Discuss with the class how these interpretations present Shylock as more than simply a stereotype.

Presenting *The Merchant of Venice* in a Condensed Time Period

Teachers need feel no frustration in condensing the student experience of a Shakespearean play into three or four weeks of classroom time (two and a half weeks in a semestered school). Increasingly, we are recognizing that a play need not be treated in complete detail. It is very important, however, to determine before you begin which scenes and sequences within the play will be treated intensively with the class and which will be selected for independent reading, class viewing, story-telling, and brief discussion.

Because of its complexities of character and intricacies of plot, *The Merchant of Venice* does not readily lend itself to a single character or single theme focus. However, it *is* appropriate for a key scenes approach. Even for classes which are not limited by time restraints, there are scenes and sequences which clearly demand more concentration and care than others. Teachers might consider the possibilities of the following approach.

Act 1 (One-third of your Shakespeare time)

Careful attention to the three important scenes of the opening act allows students to acquaint themselves with the characters and their interrelationships, to clarify the details of setting and action, and to react with some integrity to the themes and issues which are introduced early in the play. The following items deserve particular emphasis:

Scene 1 • the economy of medieval Venice
 • the friendship between Antonio and Bassanio
 • Bassanio's pursuit of Portia
 • the image of the world as a stage and life as a play

Scene 2 • the casket lottery and the dilemma it presents to Portia
 • the gallery of suitors, each drawn as a stereotype

Scene 3 • Shylock's status in Venetian society and his responses to Antonio's prejudice
 • the similarities and differences between the business ethics of Shylock and Antonio
 • the bond and its terms

Acts 2 and 3 (One-third of your Shakespeare time)

In these two acts, the loan plot and the casket plot are intricately interwoven, and the elopement plot is introduced as an added complication. Students obviously need to clarify the interconnecting details of the three plots, but their focus should remain on the continuing development of character and theme. Thus, the scenes and sequences most appropriate for intensive study are those in which character and theme predominate.

Act 2, Scenes 3–6	• Jessica's relationship with her father
	• Shylock's attitudes towards Christian "fools"
	• the masque as an opportunity for deception, theft, and escape
Act, Scene 7	• the casket inscriptions and the theme of deception (reality vs. appearance)
Act 3, Scene 1	• Shylock's reaction to his daughter's elopment and his defence of revenge
Act 3, Scene 2	• Bassanio's choice of the leaden casket
	• Portia's views on love and friendship

When time permits, students might want to explore in further depth the scenes in which Morocco and Arragon make their choice of casket. The Morocco sequence (Act 2, Scenes 1 and 7) provides another view of the prejudice of Elizabethan society.

Acts 4 and 5 (One-third of your Shakespeare time)

The obvious focus in these acts is the famous courtroom scene. This scene should not be covered in less than two full classroom hours. Students should chart the complex sequence of moves and countermoves which constitute the action of the hearing so that they understand the ways in which the scene represents the culmination of the character development and the thematic focus of the play. Students should explore the obstinacy of Shylock's demand for justice, the social dilemma of the Duke, the melancholic resignation of Antonio and Bassanio, the vindictive prejudice of Gratiano, Portia's appeal for mercy and foregiveness, her manipulation of the law, the miraculous saving of Antonio's life, and the final dispensation of "mercy" upon Shylock.

The final scene in Act 4 and the whole of Act 5 should be presented and enjoyed as pure comedy. Students may have fun with prepared readings of the final scenes, classroom productions of the fairy-tale ending, or a viewing of the final act of the BBC videotape.

As a final independent or small group activity, students should be encouraged to select and complete at least one of the "Consider the Whole Play" activities which appear at the end of the student text.

A SELECTION OF SUGGESTED CLASSROOM RESOURCES

Print Resources

Brown, Ivor. *Shakespeare in His Time.* London: Thomas Nelson, 1960. This easy introduction to Shakespeare makes important background information available to every student.

Chute, Marchette. *Shakespeare of London.* New York, E.P. Dutton, 1949. Based on documents of Shakespeare's own time, this work depicts the poet as a beacon of tolerance in a bigoted society. Senior students should appreciate it.

Grebanier, Bernard. *The Truth About Shylock.* New York: Random House, 1962.
This fascinating analysis of the play, its sources, and its historical context is a must for teachers and advanced students.

Harbage, Alfred. *As They Like It.* New York, Harper, 1961. Harbage finds evidence of Shakespeare's own generous morality in the characterization of Shylock. He provides a significant perspective for teachers.

Lelyveld, Toby. *Shylock on the Stage.* Cleveland: The Press of Western Reserve University, 1960.
Teachers and students both will be interested in this exhaustive study of how actors in four centuries have approached one of the most problematic roles in the theatre.

Sinsheimer, Herman. *Shylock: The History of a Character.* New York: The Citadel Press, 1964.
This intensive study of Shylock's character traces his development from political and social forces at work in Shakespeare's time. Like Chute, Sinsheimer concludes that the playwright's humanity outstrips his age.

Bloom, Alan. *Shakespeare's Politics.* New York: Basic Books Inc., 1964. Professor Bloom brings the critical eye of the political philosopher to his analysis. His insights will help teachers to resolve some of the seeming contradictions of the play, especially the problem of Portia's "heroic" character.

Mersand, Joseph, *et al. Teacher's Study Guide: Stereotypes in English Literature: Shylock and Fagin.* New York: B'nai Brith and the Catholic Archdiocese of New York, 1969.
This publication, available from either B'nai Brith or the Catholic Archdiocese of New York, provides a wealth of resources in the form of essays, classroom activities, and bibliographies on Shakespeare and anti-Semitism.

Of special interest to teachers:
Barnet, Sylvan, ed. *Twentieth Century Interpretations of The Merchant of Venice: A Collection of Critical Essays.* Englewood Cliffs, New Jersey: Prentice-Hall, 1970.
This critical anthology contains articles by a number of familiar Shakespearean scholars: C.L. Barber, Harley Granville-Barker, G. Wilson Knight, and Frank Kermode, amongst others. Of particular interest is a study of Biblical allusions in the play and an interpretation of the play as allegory by Barbara Lewalski. This volume also contains a chronology which puts Shakespeare's life in the context of the history of Jews in England.

Bloom, Harold, ed. *The Merchant of Venice: Modern Critical Interpretations.* New York: Chelsea House, 1986.
This most recent collection of critical articles on the play contains an especially interesting chapter by Leslie Fiedler on Shylock as stranger, suggesting that, if we wish to find the real meaning of the play, we must "descend to the level of what is most archaic in our living selves and there confront the living Shylock. . . ."

Frye, Northrop. 'Archetypal Criticism: Theory of Myths" in his *Anatomy of Criticism.* Princeton, New Jersey: Princeton University Press, 1957.
Frye's analysis of the comic pattern, "the mythos of spring," has been formative of our own perspective on Shakespeare's comedies. Whether you choose to bring the archetypal approach to your classroom or not, you will find that examining the play in the context of a consistent dramatic form will help you to interpret it.

Wilders, John ed. *The Merchant of Venice: A Casebook.* London: Macmillan, 1969.
In addition to the academic criticism you would expect in a volume of this sort, Wilders includes Nicholas Rowe's early "review" of the play (1709) and a fascinating exploration of the casket plot by Sigmund Freud (1913).

Visual Resources
(a) Videotape
> *The Merchant of Venice.* BBC Television Shakespeare, 1980. (Beta or VHS format) (150 minutes)
> This designed-for-television production is a flexible resource. The character interpretations are conventional, and the production does a good job of suggesting the Venetian setting and atmosphere.

(b) 16mm Films
> *Understanding Shakespeare: His Stagecraft.* Gateway Films, 1971.

(25 minutes)

Shakespeare of Stratford and London. National Geographic Society, 1978. (32 minutes)

Venice. Enclyclopaedia Britannica Films, 1951. (10 minutes)

Sound Recordings (LP or cassette)

The Merchant of Venice (complete). Caedmon Records.
Hugh Griffith as Shylock. Directed by Peter Wood.

The Merchant of Venice (complete). London Records.
The Marlowe Society and Professional Players.

The Merchant of Venice (abridged). Caedmon Records.
Sir Michael Redgrave as Shylock. Directed by R.D. Smith.

(c) Filmstrips

The Playhouse comes to London. Encyclopaedia Britannica Films.

Prologue to the Globe Theatre. Encyclopaedia Britannica Films.

A Day at the Globe Theatre. Encyclopaedia Britannica Films.

The Theatre and the Players (in the series *Life in Elizabethan Times*), McGraw-Hill.

Other Resources

A model of the Globe Theatre, posters, a bulletin board kit, and other classroom materials are available from The Perfection Form Company, Logan, Iowa, U.S.A. 51546

THE
MERCHANT
OF VENICE

HBJ SHAKESPEARE

THE
MERCHANT
OF VENICE

edited by
Mark Maitman
and
Ian Waldron

Harcourt Brace Jovanovich, Canada

Toronto Orlando San Diego London Sydney

Copyright © 1988 Harcourt Brace Jovanovich Canada Inc.
55 Horner Avenue, Toronto, Ontario M8Z 4X6

All rights reserved. No part of this publication may be reproduced or transmitted in any form or by any means, electronic or mechanical, without permission in writing from the publisher. Reproducing passages from this book by mimeographing or by photographic, electrostatic, or mechanical means without such written permission is an infringement of copyright law.

HBJ Shakespeare: Series Editor, Ken Roy

Canadian Cataloguing in Publication Data

Shakespeare, William, 1564–1616
  The merchant of Venice

(HBJ Shakespeare)
For use in high schools.
ISBN 0-7747-1263-5

I. Waldron, Ian. II. Title. III. Series.

PR2825.A2W34 1988   822.3'3   C88-093588-X

88 89 90 91 92 5 4 3 2

Editorial Director: Murray Lamb
Senior Editor: Lydia Fletcher
Project Editor: Elynor Kagan
Production Editor: Dick Hemingway
Designer: Michael van Elsen
Illustrators: Marika and Laszlo Gal
Cover Illustrators: Marika and Laszlo Gal
Typesetter: Q Composition
Printed in Canada by Friesen Printers

Acknowledgments

The editors and publisher acknowledge the consultants listed below for their contribution to the development of this program:

Wayne McNanny
Language Arts Consultant, Waterloo Board of Education, Kitchener, Ontario

Elana Scraba
former English Department Head, Edmonton Public School Board, Edmonton, Alberta

Nancy Steinhauer
Student, North Toronto Collegiate, Toronto Board of Education, Toronto, Ontario

To the Reader

This edition of *The Merchant of Venice* has been designed to encourage your active participation in the dramatic experience of Shakespeare's play.

Before reading each scene in the play, you will have an opportunity to explore ideas, themes, or personal experiences similar to the ones you will read about. You might want to discuss your opinions in small groups or, perhaps, record your responses in a journal.

As you begin to read each scene, a brief note will provide you with an outline of events within the scene, freeing you to think about the characters, their concerns and personalities, their relationships, and their interaction.

The notes of explanation which accompany Shakespeare's script are intended to speed your reading and enrich your enjoyment and understanding of the play. You will discover your own way of using them to your advantage. Be careful never to let them interfere with your experience of the play itself. You can always return to some of the longer historical notes after your first reading of each scene.

Each scene is followed by a set of activities related to its themes and problems. You might want to explore these activities after each scene, after a group of scenes, or at the end of each act. Whichever you decide, you will discover that many of these activities, like the ones before each scene, call for group work and personal responses.

Your study of the play will be more efficient and productive if you maintain an organized approach. With your teacher, decide on what this approach will be. It might include a notebook for answers to general questions, a personal journal or reading log, a writing folder for creative explorations and compositions, or a director's log or script book.

Now that you have some idea about how the text will be presented in the pages that follow, you are ready to experience the play.

Getting Started

Although *The Merchant of Venice* is set in medieval times, the issues and concerns which Shakespeare develops in the play are surprisingly contemporary. As you read the play, you will want to think about events in your own life and situations in the modern world that reflect the themes and ideas of the play. You might even want to take some time before you actually begin the text of the play to discuss some of the questions in small groups and record in your journal some of your classmates' responses, particularly those you find interesting or thought-provoking. Another possibility is to record your own thoughts on these issues in a series of personal journal entries.

1. In our society, friendship is valued very highly. So is money. Which do you value more? What differences in personality and behaviour do you notice between those who value friends above all else and those who value money most?

2. "Don't judge a book by its cover!" What do you think this common saying means? What personal experiences have made you more aware that appearances can be deceptive? What happens to those who put their trust in appearances?

3. It is generally agreed that children should obey their parents. Why is this so? Under what circumstances might a parent not deserve obedience from his or her children? When is a young person old enough to replace blind obedience with independent thought?

4. When many members of a society share a prejudice, they often discriminate against those who are in some way different. Have you ever been the victim of someone else's prejudice? What form did that prejudice take? How did you deal with it?

Return to these questions and your answers as you study the text. You will find that they provide you with a focus for discussing and writing about the play.

3

Dramatis Personae:
Literally, these Latin words mean "Masks of the Play." In Greek and Roman times, actors wore masks. Today and in Shakespeare's day, the title simply means "Characters."

clown:
In the Elizabethan theatre, this term was not necessarily used to describe professional comedians, but, more commonly, it referred to an uneducated rustic, a "country bumpkin," a "hick."

waiting-maid:
She waits upon (serves) her mistress.

Magnificoes:
Venetian noblemen of great influence and wealth. Their appearance, of course, would be truly "magnificent."

Gaoler:
early spelling (still used in Great Britain) for *jailer*

seat:
traditional family residence, estate

Continent:
the continent of Europe. As a set of islands, Venice itself was *not* a part of the continent.

Dramatis Personae

(Characters in the Play)

Duke of Venice
Prince of Morocco } Suitors to Portia
Prince of Arragon
Antonio, the merchant of Venice
Bassanio, his friend
Salanio
Salerio } friends to Antonio and Brassanio
Gratiano
Lorenzo, in love with Jessica
Shylock, a Jew
Tubal, a Jew, his friend
Launcelot Gobbo, a clown, servant to Shylock, afterwards to
    Bassanio
Old Gobbo, father to Launcelot
Leonardo, servant to Bassanio
Balthazar
Stephano } servants to Portia
Portia, a rich heiress
Nerissa, her waiting-maid
Jessica, daughter to Shylock
Magnificoes of Venice, Officers of the Court of Justice, Gaoler,
    Servants, and other Attendants
Scene: Partly at Venice and partly at Belmont, the seat of Portia,
    on the Continent

Act 1, Scene 1

In this scene . . .

The play begins in Venice. Antonio, a merchant and nobleman, is in low spirits. His companions assume he is worried about his trading ships, but we learn that he is concerned rather about Bassanio, his best friend. Bassanio is in debt, having wasted all of his own money and the money he has previously borrowed from Antonio. Furthermore, Bassanio now finds himself with a new concern. He has fallen in love with Portia, a wealthy and beautiful heiress. If he marries her, his financial problems will be solved. Without money, however, he cannot afford to travel to Belmont, where she lives, and become one of her many suitors.

Antonio has no money to give Bassanio, but he promises to use his reputation as an honest and reliable merchant to borrow the cash Bassanio needs to seek Portia's hand in marriage.

1 *In sooth:* in truth, truthfully; *sad:* serious, solemn, grave (not simply unhappy)

5 *I am to learn:* etc. I have yet to learn (I do not know)

6 *want-wit:* lack-wit, a person who lacks wit or intelligence

7 *Ado:* to do (that is, difficulty or trouble)

9 *argosies:* large merchant ships

10 *signiors:* gentlemen, noblemen; *burghers:* citizens; *flood:* sea

11 *pageants:* floats in a parade

12 *overpeer:* look down upon (What attitude is implied?); *petty traffickers:* small and insignificant trading boats

15 *had I:* if I had. This reversal of word order is very common in Shakespeare's plays. Watch for it again. *venture:* business "adventure", suggesting risk and uncertainty of gain or loss

16 *affections:* thoughts and feelings

18 *Plucking the grass:* to toss it into the air to see which way the wind is blowing

19 *roads:* anchorages (sheltered waters near the shore where ships may lie safely at anchor)

21 *out of doubt:* certainly

22 *wind:* breath; *broth:* soup

23 *ague:* fever

26 *flats:* sandbars

25-26 *I should not see . . . But . . . think:* if I saw . . . then I would think

27 *Andrew:* typical name for a merchant ship, used here by Salerio for the imaginary ship he creates; *dock'd:* run aground

28-29 *Vailing her high-top . . . her burial:* What happened to the ship after it ran aground?

30 *holy edifice:* altar

31 *straight:* straight away, immediately

29-31 *Should I go to church . . . and not bethink me:* if I were to go to church . . . would I not think?

32 *touching but:* simply by touching

Act 1, Scene 1

Venice. A street

Enter Antonio, Salerio, and Solanio

Antonio: In sooth, I know not why I am so sad:
  It wearies me; you say it wearies you;
  But how I caught it, found it, or came by it,
  What stuff 'tis made of, whereof it is born,
  I am to learn;   5
  And such a want-wit sadness makes of me,
  That I have much ado to know myself.
Salerio: Your mind is tossing on the ocean,
  There, where your argosies with portly sail,
  Like signiors and rich burghers on the flood,   10
  Or, as it were, the pageants of the sea,
  Do overpeer the petty traffickers,
  That curtsy to them, do them reverence,
  As they fly by them with their woven wings.
Solanio: Believe me, sir, had I such venture forth,   15
  The better part of my affections would
  Be with my hopes abroad. I should be still
  Plucking the grass to know where sits the wind;
  Peering in maps for ports, and piers, and roads;
  And every object that might make me fear   20
  Misfortune to my ventures, out of doubt
  Would make me sad.
Salerio: My wind, cooling my broth,
  Would blow me to an ague, when I thought
  What harm a wind too great might do at sea.
  I should not see the sandy hour-glass run   25
  But I should think of shallows and of flats,
  And see my wealthy Andrew dock'd in sand
  Vailing her high-top lower than her ribs
  To kiss her burial. Should I go to church
  And see the holy edifice of stone,   30
  And not bethink me straight of dangerous rocks,
  Which touching but my gentle vessel's side

33-34   *spices . . . silks:* Where would the *Andrew* have picked up this cargo, and where would she be taking it?

35   *in a word:* briefly

35-36   *but even now . . . worth nothing:* What gesture would Salerio use to illustrate his point in these lines?

38   *bechanc'd:* if it happened

41   *fortune:* good luck

42   *one bottom:* the hold of a single ship

43-44   *Nor is . . . present year:* I have not risked all my wealth on this year's voyages. Antonio uses "fortune" to suggest both luck (or chance) and wealth.

47   *Fie, fie:* Nonsense!

50   *two-headed Janus:* a Roman god with two faces, one happy and one sad

51   *fram'd:* created

52   *evermore peep . . . eyes:* have eyes that are always narrow because they are smiling

53   *parrots:* Parrots were considered to be stupid and foolish birds.

54   *vinegar aspect:* sour disposition

56   *Nestor:* the oldest and wisest of the Greek chieftains who fought in the Trojan War. His name has come to suggest the wisdom of age and experience.

57   *kinsman:* Solanio means close friend rather than relative.

64   *embrace th'occasion:* take this opportunity

67   *You grow exceeding strange:* You have almost become a stranger (that is, we hardly ever see you anymore).

68   *We'll make . . . yours:* We'll arrange our free time to fit yours.

Would scatter all her spices on the stream,
Enrobe the roaring waters with my silks;
And, in a word, but even now worth this,   35
And now worth nothing? Shall I have the thought
To think on this, and shall I lack the thought
That such a thing bechanc'd would make me sad?
But tell not me: I know Antonio
Is sad to think upon his merchandise.   40
Antonio: Believe me, no: I thank my fortune for it,
   My ventures are not in one bottom trusted,
   Nor to one place; nor is my whole estate
   Upon the fortune of this present year:
   Therefore, my merchandise makes me not sad.   45
Solanio: Why, then you are in love.
Antonio: Fie, fie!
Salerio: Not in love neither? Then let us say you are sad
   Because you are not merry: and 'twere as easy
   For you to laugh and leap, and say you are merry
   Because you are not sad. Now, by two-headed Janus,   50
   Nature hath fram'd strange fellows in her time:
   Some that will evermore peep through their eyes,
   And laugh like parrots at a bag-piper;
   And other of such vinegar aspect
   That they'll not show their teeth in way of smile,   55
   Though Nestor swear the jest be laughable.
   Enter Bassanio, Lorenzo, and Gratiano
Solanio: Here comes Bassanio, your most noble kinsman,
   Gratiano, and Lorenzo. Fare ye well:
   We leave you now with better company.
Salerio: I would have stay'd till I had made you merry,   60
   If worthier friends had not prevented me.
Antonio: Your worth is very dear in my regard.
   I take it, your own business calls on you,
   And you embrace th' occasion to depart.
Salerio: Good morrow, my good lords.   65
Bassanio: Good signiors both, when shall we laugh? say,
      when?
   You grow exceeding strange: must it be so?
Salerio: We'll make our leisures to attend on yours.
                        [*Exeunt Salerio and Solanio*]

74   *You have too much respect:* you are worrying too much

73-75   *You look . . . much care:* How does Gratiano echo the comments
          of Salerio and Solanio?

76   *marvellously:* greatly, very much

77   *hold:* consider

82   *mortifying:* dying

84   *cut in alabaster:* sculpted in marble (probably on his tomb)

85   *jaundice:* a liver disease, in Elizabethan times associated with
          bad temper

86   *peevish:* bad-tempered

88   *visages:* faces

89   *do cream and mantle:* develop a white surface scum

90-92   *And do . . . profound conceit:* and put on a show of being solemn
          in order to create an impression of being very intelligent

93   *As who:* as though he; *Oracle:* prophet. The ancient Greeks
          believed the gods spoke through the voice of an oracle. There-
          fore, the oracle spoke with great wisdom and foresight.

96-97   *only are reputed . . . nothing:* are considered to be wise only
          because they say nothing

97-99   *when I am very sure . . . brothers fools:* The Bible threatens
          damnation to those who call their brothers fools. (*Matthew*
          5:22). If these quiet people *did* speak, everyone would realize
          that they were fools.

101-102 *But fish not . . . this opinion:* Do not fish for a reputation as a
          wise man by pretending to be serious (like the fools described
          in the previous lines). The gudgeon is a small European fish
          which is easily caught; metaphorically, it means a gullible person
          (one who will believe anything).

104   *exhortation:* advice

106   *dumb:* silent, mute

Lorenzo: My Lord Bassanio, since you have found Antonio,
    We two will leave you; but, at dinner-time,   70
    I pray you, have in mind where we must meet.
Bassanio: I will not fail you.
Gratiano: You look not well, Signior Antonio;
    You have too much respect upon the world:
    They lose it that do buy it with much care.   75
    Believe me, you are marvellously chang'd.
Antonio: I hold the world but as the world, Gratiano;
    A stage where every man must play a part,
    And mine a sad one.
Gratiano: Let me play the fool:
    With mirth and laughter let old wrinkles come,   80
    And let my liver rather heat with wine
    Than my heart cool with mortifying groans.
    Why should a man, whose blood is warm within,
    Sit like his grandsire cut in alabaster,
    Sleep when he wakes, and creep into the jaundice   85
    By being peevish? I tell thee what, Antonio—
    I love thee, and 'tis my love that speaks—
    There are a sort of men whose visages
    Do cream and mantle like a standing pond,
    And do a wilful stillness entertain,   90
    With purpose to be dress'd in an opinion
    Of wisdom, gravity, profound conceit,
    As who should say, 'I am Sir Oracle,
    And when I ope my lips, let no dog bark!'
    O my Antonio, I do know of these   95
    That therefore only are reputed wise
    For saying nothing; when, I am very sure,
    If they should speak, would almost damn those ears
    Which, hearing them, would call their brothers fools.
    I'll tell thee more of this another time: 100
    But fish not, with this melancholy bait,
    For this fool-gudgeon, this opinion.
    Come, good Lorenzo. Fare ye well awhile:
    I'll end my exhortation after dinner.
Lorenzo: Well, we will leave you then till dinner-time.   105
    I must be one of these same dumb wise men,
    For Gratiano never lets me speak.

110   *I'll grow . . . this gear:* your nonsensical argument has convinced me to talk more

111   *commendable:* praiseworthy

112   *neat's tongue dried:* smoked ox-tongue; *maid not vendible:* unattractive young girl (with nothing to make her attractive other than the fact that she does not talk too much)

116   *chaff:* waste husks. The husks must be removed from wheat before it can be used to make flour.

117   *ere:* before

120   *pilgrimage:* a journey made to a holy place. The use of the word here implies that the lady in question is especially worthy of respect or reverence.

124-125 *By something . . . continuance:* by living beyond my means

126-127 *Nor do I . . . noble rate:* and I do not complain about my loss of the rich life

128   *to come fairly off from:* to repay fully and properly

129   *prodigal:* wasteful, extravagant

130   *gag'd:* engaged, bound, obligated

132   *warranty:* permission, agreement

133   *unburden:* reveal; *plots:* plans

138   *my extremest means:* "my last penny"

139   *occasions:* needs

140   *shaft:* arrow

141   *his fellow:* its companion (that is, another arrow)

142   *advised:* careful

143   *adventuring:* risking (compare line 15 and lines 41-44)

144   *oft:* often

145   *innocence:* childlike sincerity

Gratiano: Well, keep me company but two years more,
 Thou shalt not know the sound of thine own tongue.
Antonio: Fare you well: I'll grow a talker for this gear.   110
Gratiano: Thanks, i' faith; for silence is only commendable
 In a neat's tongue dried and a maid not vendible.
         [Exeunt Gratiano and Lorenzo]
Antonio: Is that anything now?
Bassanio: Gratiano speaks an infinite deal of nothing, more
  than any man in all Venice. His reasons are as two   115
  grains of wheat hid in two bushels of chaff: you shall
  seek all day ere you find them, and when you have
  them, they are not worth the search.
Antonio: Well, tell me now, what lady is the same
 To whom you swore a secret pilgrimage,   120
 That you today promis'd to tell me of?
Bassanio: 'Tis not unknown to you, Antonio,
 How much I have disabled mine estate,
 By something showing a more swelling port
 Than my faint means would grant continuance: 125
 Nor do I now make moan to be abridg'd
 From such a noble rate; but my chief care
 Is, to come fairly off from the great debts
 Wherein my time, something too prodigal,
 Hath left me gag'd. To you, Antonio,   130
 I owe the most, in money and in love;
 And from your love I have a warranty
 To unburden all my plots and purposes
 How to get clear of all the debts I owe.
Antonio: I pray you, good Bassanio, let me know it;   135
 And if it stand, as you yourself still do,
 Within the eye of honour, be assur'd,
 My purse, my person, my extremest means,
 Lie all unlock'd to your occasions.
Bassanio: In my school-days, when I had lost one shaft,   140
 I shot his fellow of the self-same flight
 The self-same way with more advised watch,
 To find the other forth; and by adventuring both,
 I oft found both. I urge this childhood proof,
 Because what follows is pure innocence.   145
 I owe you much, and (like a wilful youth)

148   *self:* same

150-151 *or . . . or:* either . . . or

151   *latter hazard:* second risk (that is, a second loan)

152   *rest:* remain

154   *circumstance:* "beating around the bush"

155   *out of doubt:* certainly

156   *In making question . . . uttermost:* by questioning my willingness
         to do all I can

160   *prest:* committed, ready

161   *lady richly left:* heiress

162   *fair:* beautiful. This is almost always Shakespeare's meaning,
         for human beauty in the Renaissance was considered to require
         light skin and blonde hair.

165   *nothing:* in no way

166   *To Cato's . . . Portia:* Cato's daughter, also named Portia, was
         married to Brutus, the Roman aristocrat. She had a reputation
         for beauty and wisdom.

170   *golden fleece:* the fabulous golden woolskin which Jason, the
         Greek hero-adventurer, and his Argonauts brought from Col-
         chis (a country on the Black Sea) back to Greece. In Elizabethan
         England, the fleece represented the success or fortune sought
         by sea-faring merchants. The use of "fleece" here points to both
         the beauty of Portia's hair and her wealth.

171   *seat:* home; *strand:* beach, shore

173   *means:* that is, money

174   *rival:* equal

175   *presages:* predicts

178   *commodity:* merchandise (to serve as a guarantee for a loan)

181   *rack'd:* stretched (as on the rack, an instrument of torture which
         stretched the victim's body over a wooden frame, pulling limbs
         out of joint).

182   *To furnish thee to Belmont:* to equip you for your journey to
         Belmont

184   *no question make:* am sure

185   *of my trust or for my sake:* either on the basis of my credit or
         as a personal favour to me

That which I owe is lost; but if you please
To shoot another arrow that self way
Which you did shoot the first, I do not doubt,
(As I will watch the aim) or to find both,   150
Or bring your latter hazard back again
And thankfully rest debtor for the first.
Antonio: You know me well, and herein spend but time
To wind about my love with circumstance;
And out of doubt you do me now more wrong   155
In making question of my uttermost
Than if you had made waste of all I have.
Then do but say to me what I should do
That in your knowledge may by me be done,
And I am prest unto it: therefore speak.   160
Bassanio: In Belmont is a lady richly left,
And she is fair, and, fairer than that word,
Of wondrous virtues: sometimes from her eyes
I did receive fair speechless messages:
Her name is Portia; nothing undervalu'd   165
To Cato's daughter, Brutus' Portia;
Nor is the wide world ignorant of her worth,
For the four winds blow in from every coast
Renowned suitors; and her sunny locks
Hang on her temples like a golden fleece;   170
Which makes her seat of Belmont Colchi's strand,
And many Jasons come in quest of her.
O my Antonio, had I but the means
To hold a rival place with one of them,
I have a mind presages me such thrift   175
That I should questionless be fortunate.
Antonio: Thou know'st that all my fortunes are at sea;
Neither have I money, nor commodity
To raise a present sum: therefore go forth,
Try what my credit can in Venice do: 180
That shall be rack'd, even to the uttermost,
To furnish thee to Belmont, to fair Portia.
Go, presently inquire, and so will I,
Where money is, and I no question make
To have it of my trust or for my sake.   *[Exeunt]* 185

Act 1, Scene 1: Activities

1. Shakespeare wrote his plays to be seen and heard, not to be read. When we read his lines silently, we miss the gestures, facial expressions, and vocal inflections which actors use to bring the lines to life. Use lines such as the following to investigate ways actors might interpret the script.

   a) Let me play the fool . . .
   For this fool-gudgeon, this opinion.   (lines 79-102)

   In this speech, Gratiano ridicules peevish old men and pompous fools with an exaggerated impersonation of their movements and voices. Act out the possibilities of this speech with your partner.

   b) In my school-days, when I had lost one shaft . . .
   And thankfully rest debtor for the first.
   (lines 140-152)

   Deliver this speech to your partner as you think Bassanio would do it. Remember that Bassanio tries to *demonstrate* his argument, and to charm Antonio with a childlike sincerity.

   Record your versions of your speeches for presentation and comparison. Compare your interpretations with those recorded by professionals.

2. In the opening lines of the play (lines 1-40) Solanio and Salerio create images of ships at sea, of dangerous weather, and of silk and spice. These images all help to build an impression of business in medieval times.

   Suppose that you have been asked to update this play to modern times. Create a list of activities, places, and objects which would be appropriate to a play about business in today's world. Describe how your list reveals important changes in business practice since medieval times.

3. On the stage of life, Gratiano wishes to play the fool (lines 79-102). What recommendations does he make to one who might also like to play this role?

What role would you like to play in life? Write a brief description of the role and how it should be played. Some suggestions of the roles are the ones such as the following: star athlete, scholar, politician, social butterfly.

4. Examine the speech in which Bassanio reveals his feelings about Portia (lines 161-176). Make a list of words and phrases that describe Bassanio as he appears to you in this speech. Take care to examine his reasons for pursuing Portia and look carefully at his reference to the story of Jason and the golden fleece.

Review your list as you continue reading. Make additions and changes as you learn more about Bassanio.

5. Review Antonio's conversation with Bassanio (lines 119-185), making note of characteristics which contrast with Bassanio's personality.

Begin with Antonio's choice of image in line 120 to determine differences in their values. Prepare a list of words and phrases that describe Antonio as he appears to you in this conversation. Change and add to this list as you learn more about Antonio.

6. How do you feel when somebody asks you for money and how do you react? Assume that Antonio and Bassanio are living in the present. What circumstances might lead Bassanio to ask Antonio for money? Would the request change their relationship in any way?

For the next scene . . .

Recall a situation in which you felt you had no freedom of choice. How did you feel? What did you do?

Act 1, Scene 2

In this scene . . .

Portia and Nerissa, her maid and friend, discuss the test of character which Portia's father devised to find a suitable husband for his daughter. According to her father's will, each of Portia's suitors has to choose one of three caskets. The first casket is made of gold, the second casket is made of silver, and the third is made of lead. The man who is intelligent enough to make the right choice will marry Portia. Portia is clearly worried about the outcome of the lottery. Nerissa entertains her by cataloguing the parade of suitors who have already come to Belmont. Portia ridicules them all. At the end of the scene, Nerissa reminds Portia of her special interest in Bassanio, who once visited Belmont.

1   *By my troth:* to tell the truth

5   *aught:* anything; *surfeit:* eat and drink to excess, overindulge

7   *mean:* insignificant. Compare the modern phrase "no mean feat."

8   *seated in the mean:* placed in the centre (between extremes). Notice the pun on the word *mean* in lines 7 and 8. *superfluity:* excess; *comes by:* acquires, gets

9   *competency:* moderation

10   *sentences:* opinions, proverbs (here, advice)

13   *had been:* would have been

14   *divine:* preacher

18   *blood:* passions, emotions; *hot temper:* passionate, high-spirited, youthful temperament; *leaps o'er:* leaps over, ignores

19   *hare:* rabbit

20   *meshes:* nets. In Elizabethan times, hares were hunted on foot with small-meshed nets. *counsel:* advice

24   *curbed:* restricted, controlled. Notice Portia's pun on *will* in this same line.

27-33 *Your father . . . rightly love:* Nerissa suggests that this lottery is not merely a game of chance.

Scene 2

Belmont. A room in Portia's house

Enter Portia and Nerissa

Portia: By my troth, Nerissa, my little body is aweary of
   this great world.
Nerissa: You would be, sweet madam, if your miseries were
   in the same abundance as your good fortunes are: and
   yet, for aught I see, they are as sick that surfeit with   5
   too much as they that starve with nothing. It is no
   mean happiness therefore, to be seated in the mean:
   superfluity comes sooner by white hairs, but
   competency lives longer.
Portia: Good sentences, and well pronounced.   10
Nerissa: They would be better if well followed.
Portia: If to do were as easy as to know what were good to
   do, chapels had been churches, and poor men's
   cottages princes' palaces. It is a good divine that follows
   his own instructions: I can easier teach twenty what   15
   were good to be done, than be one of the twenty to
   follow mine own teaching. The brain may devise laws
   for the blood, but a hot temper leaps o'er a cold decree:
   such a hare is madness (the youth), to skip o'er the
   meshes of good counsel (the cripple). But this reasoning   20
   is not in the fashion to choose me a husband. O me,
   the word 'choose'! I may neither choose who I would
   nor refuse who I dislike; so is the will of a living
   daughter curbed by the will of a dead father. Is it not
   hard, Nerissa, that I cannot choose one, nor refuse   25
   none?
Nerissa: Your father was ever virtuous, and holy men at
   their death have good inspirations; therefore, the lottery
   that he hath devised in these three chests of gold,
   silver, and lead, whereof who chooses his meaning   30

37   *level at:* try to guess

38   *Neapolitan:* from Naples, Italy

40   *appropriation:* compliment

41   *parts:* qualities

43   *smith:* blacksmith. What insult is Portia implying? *County Palatine:* Count Palatine was the title given to a nobleman who had complete right to rule his own territory within a state or kingdom.

45   *as who should say:* as much as to say; *And:* if

49   *unmannerly:* unsuitable, inappropriate

50   *death's head:* skull

57   *he is . . . no man:* he has no personality; *throstle:* thrush, an English songbird; *a-capering:* dancing, leaping

61-62   *requite him:* return his love

70   *dumb-show:* performance in mime; *suited:* dressed

chooses you, will, no doubt, never be chosen by any
rightly but one who you shall rightly love. But what
warmth is there in your affection towards any of these
princely suitors that are already come?

Portia: I pray thee, over-name them, and as thou namest   35
them, I will describe them; and, according to my
description, level at my affection.

Nerissa: First there is the Neapolitan prince.

Portia: Ay, that's a colt indeed, for he doth nothing but
talk of his horse; and he makes it a great appropriation   40
to his own good parts that he can shoe him himself.
I am much afeard my lady his mother played false with
a smith.

Nerissa: Then is there the County Palatine.

Portia: He doth nothing but frown, as who should say, 'And   45
you will not have me, choose.' He hears merry tales,
and smiles not: I fear he will prove the weeping
philosopher when he grows old, being so full of
unmannerly sadness in his youth. I had rather be
married to a death's-head with a bone in his mouth than   50
to either of these. God defend me from these two!

Nerissa: How say you by the French lord, Monsieur Le Bon?

Portia: God made him, and therefore let him pass for a
man. In truth, I know it is a sin to be mocker; but, he!
why, he hath a horse better than the Neapolitan's, a   55
better bad habit of frowning than the Count Palatine;
he is every man in no man; if a throstle sing, he falls
straight a-capering; he will fence with his own shadow.
If I should marry him, I should marry twenty
husbands: if he would despise me, I would forgive   60
him, for if he loves me to madness, I shall never requite
him.

Nerissa: What say you, then, to Falconbridge, the young
baron of England?

Portia: You know I say nothing to him, for he understands   65
not me, nor I him: he hath neither Latin, French, nor
Italian; and you will come into the court and swear
that I have a poor pennyworth in the English. He is a
proper man's picture, but, alas! who can converse
with a dumb-show? How oddly he is suited! I think he   70

71   *doublet:* tunic. The nearest modern equivalent would be a tightly fitted suit jacket; *hose:* stockings

76   *borrowed a box of the ear of:* was punched by

78   *surety:* supporter (guarantor of a loan); *sealed under for another:* promised to repay (retaliate)

75-79   *That he hath . . . for another:* In Shakespeare's time, many people in Scotland and France shared a common dislike of the English. Indeed, Mary Queen of Scots was supported by many French people in her claim to the English throne.

85-86   *And . . . fell:* if the worst should happen

86   *make shift:* make do, manage

90   *should refuse:* would be refusing

92   *Rhenish wine:* white wine from the Rhine Valley in Germany

95   *ere:* before

99   *suit:* courtship

101   *imposition:* command

102   *Sibylla:* a prophetess in ancient times, famous for her extreme old age as well as her predictions; *chaste:* pure, virgin

103   *Diana:* the Roman goddess of feminine virtue and purity

105   *dote on:* long for

bought his doublet in Italy, his round hose in France,
his bonnet in Germany, and his behaviour
everywhere.

Nerissa: What think you of the Scottish lord, his neighbour?

Portia: That he hath a neighbourly charity in him, for he   75
borrowed a box of the ear of the Englishman, and swore
he would pay him again when he was able: I think
the Frenchman became his surety and sealed under for
another.

Nerissa: How like you the young German, the Duke of   80
Saxony's nephew?

Portia: Very vilely in the morning, when he is sober, and
most vilely in the afternoon, when he is drunk: when
he is best, he is a little worse than a man, and when
he is worst, he is little better than a beast. And the   85
worst fall that ever fell, I hope I shall make shift to
go without him.

Nerissa: If he should offer to choose, and choose the right
casket, you should refuse to perform your father's
will, if you should refuse to accept him.   90

Portia: Therefore, for fear of the worst, I pray thee, set a
deep glass of Rhenish wine on the contrary casket,
for, if the devil be within and that temptation without,
I know he will choose it. I will do anything, Nerissa,
ere I will be married to a sponge.   95

Nerissa: You need not fear, lady, the having any of
these lords: they have acquainted me with their
determinations; which is, indeed, to return to their
home and to trouble you with no more suit, unless you
may be won by some other sort than your father's   100
imposition depending on the caskets.

Portia: If I live to be as old as Sibylla, I will die as chaste
as Diana, unless I be obtained by the manner of my
father's will. I am glad this parcel of wooers are so
reasonable, for there is not one among them but I dote   105
on his very absence, and I pray God grant them a fair
departure.

Nerissa: Do you not remember, lady, in your father's time,
a Venetian, a scholar and a soldier, that came hither
in company of the Marquis of Montferrat?   110

124 *condition:* character

125 *complexion of a devil:* In medieval and Renaissance times, the devil was thought to have dark skin. The association of black skin with evil is yet another indication of the prejudice of Shakespeare's day.

126 *shrive me:* hear my confession (as a priest would)

127 *sirrah:* a term used by older persons to address men and boys of less authority.

Portia: Yes, yes: it was Bassanio—as I think so was he called.
True, madam: he of all the men that ever my foolish eyes
looked upon, was the best deserving a fair lady.
Portia: I remember him well, and I remember him worthy
of thy praise.   115
Enter a Servant
How now, what news?
Servant: The four strangers seek for you, madam, to take
their leave; and there is a forerunner come from a fifth,
the Prince of Morocco, who brings word the prince   120
his master will be here tonight.
Portia: If I could bid the fifth welcome with so good heart
as I can bid the other four farewell, I should be glad
of his approach: if he have the condition of a saint
and the complexion of a devil, I had rather he should   125
shrive me than wive me.
Come, Nerissa. [*To Attendant*] Sirrah, go before. Whiles
we shut the gate upon one wooer, another knocks at
the door.
                                                            [*Exeunt*]

Act 1, Scene 2: Activities

1. If Nerissa and Portia were friends today, how would Nerissa express the piece of advice offered in lines 3-9? As Nerissa, write your advice either as a personal note to Portia or as it might appear in the advice column of a daily newspaper.

2. Portia feels trapped by her father's will. Adopting the role of her father, write the letter which he might have left her, explaining why the will is so strict and confining. Try to justify Nerissa's claim that the lottery was a "good inspiration."

3. Throughout this scene, what evidence can you find to suggest that Nerissa is confidante and friend as well as maid to Portia? Compare your findings with those of others in the class.

4. Prejudices are beliefs we hold about groups of people, especially racial, cultural, or national groups different from ourselves. Prejudices are like very dark glasses we wear when looking at individual members of these groups: they colour what we will see before we have seen it; they may even blind us totally to what is there. Prejudices force us to assume that what we believe about a group must be true of every individual in that group.

   When Portia describes her suitors, she reduces each one to a comic stereotype of his nationality.

   a) With a partner, make a list of the six suitors described in this scene, and outline Portia's observations about each. As you review the list together, speculate upon the prejudices Shakespeare's audience might have held about French, German, and Scottish people.

   b) What features of Portia's descriptions of the suitors make you suspect that she is not accurately describing the European noblemen she had met, but is embellishing her descriptions to match her prejudices? (Consider, for example, whether a young German aristocrat would travel to Belmont only to be influenced by a glass of wine, or whether a French gentleman would dance to the song of a bird.) Generate a short list of the common features of Portia's speech (such as hyperbole, insult, biased selection of detail, uncomplimentary metaphor) that suggest she is "colouring" her descriptions.

c) Are you willing to forgive Portia her prejudice in this scene? Explain your reasons in a personal journal entry.

d) What are the dangers of seeing people as stereotypes rather than as individuals? Are some forms of prejudice more dangerous than others? Write your answers, with reasons, in your personal journal.

5. Portia has met each of her suitors only once. In pairs, write a script for Portia's interview with one of her suitors as it really happened. In deciding what the suitor should say, pay attention to Portia's description of him, but remember her possible prejudices.

6. By the end of this scene, we suspect that Portia is in love with Bassanio. What obstacles can you see to their eventual marriage? In your notebook, predict how these obstacles might be overcome.

For the next scene . . .

How do you know who your real friends are? What are the essential characteristics of a good friend? Would you be prepared to make commitments or take risks for a good friend? What risks would you be *un*willing to take for this friend?

Act 1, Scene 3

In this scene . . .

Bassanio and Antonio have come to borrow money from Shylock, the Jewish moneylender. Shylock can raise the amount required, but he seems unwilling to lend Antonio money because Antonio has insulted him so often in the past. Shylock and Antonio argue about the morality of lending money for profit, and it appears that they will not resolve their argument. Shylock eventually agrees to lend Antonio the money and, as a show of friendship, offers the loan interest-free. However, Shylock asks that Antonio promise to repay the loan with a pound of his flesh if he cannot provide the cash. Antonio immediately agrees despite Bassanio's protests. Antonio is sure that his ships will return a month before he has to repay the loan and that his life will not be in danger.

Shylock the Jew: The label attached to Shylock in the stage direction introduces the character as a stereotype. Shakespeare's audience would have immediately recognized Shylock as a Jew by his conventional stage costume and makeup. Their familiarity with the stereotype of the Jew and their own uninformed prejudice (there were no Jews in England at this time) would lead them to expect a character who displays a stereotypical set of values and code of behaviour.

1   *ducats:* gold coins, legal currency in Venice during the medieval and Renaissance periods. In modern terms, a ducat would be worth four or five dollars.

5   *bound:* legally responsible, as the guarantor of the loan

7   *stead:* help

13   *imputation:* suggestion, charge

16   *sufficient:* of adequate means or wealth; *his means are in supposition:* his money is tied up in uncertain investments

18   *Rialto:* the business district of Venice, named for the Rialto Bridge, on which many of the moneylenders ("bankers") and trading merchants conducted their business

20   *squandered:* scattered unwisely

23   *pirates:* How would Shylock pronounce this word to make his pun?

24   *notwithstanding:* nonetheless, in spite of this

25   *bond:* contract (by which two parties are legally bound)

Scene 3

Venice. A public place

*Enter Bassanio with Shylock
the Jew*

Shylock: Three thousand ducats; well.
Bassanio: Ay, sir, for three months.
Shylock: For three months; well.
Bassanio: For the which, as I told you, Antonio shall be
    bound.   5
Shylock: Antonio shall become bound; well.
Bassanio: May you stead me? Will you pleasure me? Shall
    I know your answer?
Shylock: Three thousand ducats, for three months, and
    Antonio bound.   10
Bassanio: Your answer to that?
Shylock: Antonio is a good man.
Bassanio: Have you heard any imputation to the contrary?
Shylock: Ho, no, no, no, no; my meaning in saying he is
    a good man is to have you understand me that he is   15
    sufficient. Yet his means are in supposition: he hath
    an argosy bound to Tripolis, another to the Indies; I
    understand moreover, upon the Rialto, he hath a
    third at Mexico, a fourth for England, and other
    ventures he hath squandered abroad. But ships are   20
    but boards, sailors but men: there be land-rats and
    water-rats, water-thieves and land-thieves—I mean
    pirates—and then there is the peril of waters, winds,
    and rocks. The man is, notwithstanding, sufficient.
    Three thousand ducats; I think I may take his bond.   25
Bassanio: Be assured you may.
Shylock: I will be assured I may; and, that I may be assured,
    I will bethink me. May I speak with Antonio?
Bassanio: If it please you to dine with us.

30-31   *to eat of . . . devil into:* to eat pork into which Jesus cast devils in order to restore a madman to sanity. (See *Mark* 5:1-13.) In fact, Jews are forbidden to eat pork by the laws of the Old Testament, written long before the time of Jesus (*Leviticus* 11:7).

37   *fawning publican:* cringing, flattering tax collector. In the Roman provinces the collection of taxes was assigned to local people, who profited by squeezing money out of their own countrymen. The image of the publican may be one of the sources of the stereotype of the money-hungry Jew. Shylock would delight in applying this image to Antonio the Christian.

39   *simplicity:* stupidity

40   *gratis:* free (of interest). In 1258, a decree by Pope Alexander IV had barred Christians from charging interest on loans. Ironically, this provided an opportunity for some Jews, who were suffering under extreme conditions, to make a living. They could not move about freely, could not own land, could not work for any government, but those who had managed to amass some capital were now sought out as the only "professional bankers" in Europe. As non-Christians, they were unaffected by the Pope's ban on interest.

41   *usance:* interest

42   *catch . . . upon the hip:* a metaphor from the sport of wrestling.

43   *ancient grudge I bear him:* long-standing resentment I feel for him. The phrase suggests both the personal conflict between Shylock and Antonio and the religious tension between Christians and Jews, which began shortly after the death of Jesus.

46-47   *thrift . . . interest:* in this context, both words mean *profit.* Shylock, who lives, or "thrives," as a moneylender, prefers the word with the more positive connotations. Antonio's term, *interest,* may imply "self-interest" or "greed."

47   *tribe:* the Jewish people

51   *gross:* total

54   *But soft:* the equivalent of the modern "Hang on! Wait a minute!"

55   *Rest you fair:* a polite greeting

57   *albeit:* although

58   *excess:* interest, profit

59   *ripe:* immediate; *wants:* needs

60   *possess'd:* informed, aware

61   *would:* want

Shylock: Yes, to smell pork; to eat of the habitation which   30
    your prophet the Nazarite conjured the devil into. I
    will buy with you, sell with you, talk with you, walk
    with you, and so following; but I will not eat with
    you, drink with you, nor pray with you. What news
    on the Rialto? Who is he comes here?   35
   Enter Antonio
Bassanio: This is Signior Antonio.
Shylock: [*Aside*] How like a fawning publican he looks!
    I hate him for he is a Christian;
    But more for that in low simplicity
    He lends out money gratis, and brings down   40
    The rate of usance here with us in Venice.
    If I can catch him once upon the hip,
    I will feed fat the ancient grudge I bear him.
    He hates our sacred nation, and he rails,
    Even there where merchants most do congregate,   45
    On me, my bargains, and my well-won thrift,
    Which he calls interest. Cursed be my tribe,
    If I forgive him!
Bassanio: Shylock, do you hear?
Shylock: I am debating of my present store,
    And, by the near guess of my memory,   50
    I cannot instantly raise up the gross
    Of full three thousand ducats. What of that?
    Tubal, a wealthy Hebrew of my tribe,
    Will furnish me. But soft! how many months
    Do you desire? [*To Antonio*] Rest you fair, good signior;   55
    Your worship was the last man in our mouths.
Antonio: Shylock, albeit I neither lend nor borrow
    By taking nor by giving of excess,
    Yet, to supply the ripe wants of my friend,
    I'll break a custom. [*To Bassanio*] Is he yet possess'd   60
    How much ye would?
Shylock: Ay, ay, three thousand ducats.
Antonio: And for three months.
Shylock: I had forgot; three months; you told me so.
    Well, then, your bond; and let me see—but here you;
    Methought you said, you neither lend nor borrow   65
    Upon advantage.

67   *Jacob:* grandson ("third possessor," line 70) of Abraham (Abram), the father of the Jewish people

69   *As his wise mother . . . behalf:* thanks to the intervention of his clever mother. Rebekah had devised a scheme which allowed Jacob to receive the blessing of his father, Isaac, in the place of his older half-brother, Esau (*Genesis* 27). Shylock's digression on the ancestry of his people leaves Antonio and Bassanio impatient.

73   *mark:* take note of

74   *compromis'd:* agreed

75   *eanlings:* newborn lambs; *pied:* spotted

76   *hire:* property; *rank:* ready for mating

78   *work of generation:* conception

79   *in the act:* taking place, underway

80   *pill'd:* peeled; *wands:* sticks

81   *in the doing . . . kind:* in imitation of the natural process

82   *fulsome:* lustful, rank (as above in line 76)

84   *fall:* give birth to; *parti-coloured:* multi-coloured

85   *thrive:* make a profit

87   *venture:* outcome; *serv'd for:* was not responsible for

90   *Was this inserted . . . good:* Did you tell this story to justify your lending of money at interest?

92   *I make it breed:* by lending money at interest, Shylock makes more money.

94   *cite:* recite; *for his purpose:* to justify his own actions

99   *goodly:* a contraction of "good-like," suggesting the *appearance* of goodness

101   *beholding to you:* in your debt

102   *oft:* often

103   *rated:* berated, insulted

104   *usances:* usury, money-lending at interest

Antonio: I do never use it.
Shylock: When Jacob graz'd his uncle Laban's sheep—
    This Jacob from our holy Abram was,
    As his wise mother wrought in his behalf,
    The third possessor: ay, he was the third—   70
Antonio: And what of him? did he take interest?
Shylock: No, not take interest; not, as you would say,
    Directly interest: mark what Jacob did.
    When Laban and himself were compromis'd,
    That all the eanlings which were streak'd and pied   75
    Should fall as Jacob's hire, the ewes, being rank,
    In end of autumn turned to the rams;
    And, when the work of generation was
    Between these woolly breeders in the act,
    The skilful shepherd pill'd me certain wands,   80
    And, in the doing of the deed of kind,
    He stuck them up before the fulsome ewes,
    Who, then conceiving, did in eaning time
    Fall parti-colour'd lambs, and those were Jacob's.
    This was a way to thrive, and he was blest: 85
    And thrift is blessing, if men steal it not.
Antonio: This was a venture, sir, that Jacob serv'd for;
    A thing not in his power to bring to pass,
    But sway'd and fashion'd by the hand of heaven.
    Was this inserted to make interest good?   90
    Or is your gold and silver ewes and rams?
Shylock: I cannot tell; I make it breed as fast:
    But note me, signior.—
Antonio: Mark you this, Bassanio,
    The devil can cite Scripture for his purpose.
    An evil soul, producing holy witness,   95
    Is like a villain with a smiling cheek,
    A goodly apple rotten at the heart.
    O what a goodly outside falsehood hath!
Shylock: Three thousand ducats; 'tis a good round sum.
    Three months from twelve: then, let me see, the rate—   100
Antonio: Well, Shylock, shall we be beholding to you?
Shylock: Signior Antonio, many a time and oft
    In the Rialto you have rated me
    About my moneys and my usances:

105   *still:* always

107   *misbeliever:* literally, wrong-believer; from Antonio's point of view, a heretic or non-Christian

109   *gaberdine:* loose upper garment. Though it was not the required practice in Venice, Jews elsewhere were restricted by law to a prescribed costume. As early as 1412, for example, Jews in Spain had to wear long robes over their clothes. The Jews had been expelled from England in 1290 and would not be readmitted until 1654; however, in Elizabethan theatres, there would have been a standard, recognizable Jew's costume.

111   *Go to:* Renaissance equivalent of the modern "Get lost!"

113   *void your rheum:* spit

114   *spurn:* kick; *stranger cur:* unfamiliar mongrel dog

115   *suit:* request, demand. What then is a *suitor*? a *lawsuit*?

119   *in a bondman's key:* with the voice of a begging slave

120   *with bated breath:* hesitantly

129-130 *for when did friendship . . . friend:* for when did a friend make a profit on a loan to a friend? Christians considered money (*metal*) to be sterile (*barren*) because it was used as a means of exchange and never intended to be increased by interest (*breed*). The authority for this Christian doctrine is not the Bible, but the Greek philosopher Aristotle.

132   *break:* go broke (and fail to honour his bond); *with better face:* without appearing unfriendly (or, perhaps, simply *happily*)

133   *exact:* collect

134   *would be:* would like to be

136   *doit:* small Dutch coin (a "penny")

137   *usance:* interest

140   *notary:* person authorized to draw up contracts; *seal:* Even today, a contract must bear a legal imprint or *seal* to be considered official.

141   *single bond:* a contract naming Antonio as the sole or single debtor to Shylock. Who then is *not* legally responsible for repayment? *in a merry sport:* as a joke

Still have I borne it with a patient shrug, 105
For sufferance is the badge of all our tribe.
You call me misbeliever, cut-throat dog,
And spit upon my Jewish gaberdine,
And all for use of that which is mine own.
Well then, it now appears you need my help: 110
Go to then; you come to me, and you say,
'Shylock, we would have moneys:' you say so;
You, that did void your rheum upon my beard,
And foot me as you spurn a stranger cur
Over your threshold. Moneys is your suit. 115
What should I say to you? Should I not say,
'Hath a dog money? Is it possible
A cur can lend three thousand ducats?' or
Shall I bend low, and in a bondman's key,
With bated breath, and whispering humbleness, 120
Say this:
'Fair sir, you spat on me on Wednesday last;
You spurn'd me such a day; another time
You call'd me dog—and for these courtesies
I'll lend you thus much moneys'? 125
Antonio: I am as like to call thee so again,
To spit on thee again, to spurn thee too.
If thou wilt lend this money, lend it not
As to thy friends, for when did friendship take
A breed for barren metal of his friend? 130
But lend it rather to thine enemy;
Who if he break, thou may'st with better face
Exact the penalty.
Shylock: Why, look you, how you storm!
I would be friends with you, and have your love,
Forget the shames that you have stain'd me with, 135
Supply your present wants, and take no doit
Of usance for my moneys, and you'll not hear me:
This is kind I offer.
Bassanio: This were kindness.
Shylock: This kindness will I show.
Go with me to a notary, seal me there 140
Your single bond; and, in a merry sport,
If you repay me not on such a day,

144   *Express'd in the condition:* stated in the terms of the contract; *forfeit:* penalty

145   *Be nominated for:* be stated as; *equal:* exact

145-146 *pound Of your fair flesh:* Shylock's proposal, while unusual, is certainly not original. Although scholars have not been able to pinpoint the exact source of Shakespeare's idea, a great number and variety of European tales and stories feature such a penalty for default of a loan. (Eyes, ears, noses, and feet were also popular.) Roman law actually allowed several creditors to divide a debtor's body among themselves. Note, however, that Jewish law does *not* allow the taking of a debtor's life as punishment for default (*Leviticus* 25:39). *fair:* light, hence beautiful. Shylock's pun is clearly ironic.

148   *Content, in faith:* Indeed, I agree.

151   *dwell in my necessity:* remain in need or debt

152   *forfeit:* have to pay

154   *return:* revenue from the merchandise his ships are carrying

157   *hard:* cruel; *suspect:* to be suspicious of

160   *exaction:* collection

162   *estimable:* valued

166   *I pray you wrong me not:* I beg you not to do me wrong (by misinterpreting my kindly motives)

170   *purse:* put into my purse; *straight:* immediately

171   *in the fearful guard:* under the doubtful protection

172   *unthrifty knave:* careless servant (a rascal)

174   *Hie thee:* hurry; *gentle:* kind. The words *gentle* and *Gentile* (non-Jewish) were frequently pronounced and spelled in the same way during Elizabethan times. This pun is used several times in the play by the Christian characters, usually to mock Shylock.

In such a place, such sum or sums as are
Express'd in the condition, let the forfeit
Be nominated for an equal pound   145
Of your fair flesh, to be cut off and taken
In what part of your body pleaseth me.
Antonio: Content, in faith: I'll seal to such a bond,
And say there is much kindness in the Jew.
Bassanio: You shall not seal to such a bond for me: 150
I'll rather dwell in my necessity.
Antonio: Why, fear not, man, I will not forfeit it:
Within these two months, that's a month before
This bond expires, I do expect return
Of thrice three times the value of this bond.   155
Shylock: O father Abram, what these Christians are,
Whose own hard dealings teaches them suspect
The thoughts of others! Pray you, tell me this:
If he should break his day, what should I gain
By the exaction of the forfeiture?   160
A pound of man's flesh, taken from a man,
Is not so estimable, profitable neither,
As flesh of muttons, beefs, or goats. I say,
To buy his favour, I extend this friendship:
If he will take it, so; if not, adieu;   165
And, for my love, I pray you wrong me not.
Antonio: Yes, Shylock, I will seal unto this bond.
Shylock: Then meet me forthwith at the notary's;
Give him direction for this merry bond.
And I will go and purse the ducats straight,   170
See to my house, left in the fearful guard
Of an unthrifty knave, and presently
I'll be with you.   [*Exit Shylock*]
Antonio: Hie thee, gentle Jew.
The Hebrew will turn Christian: he grows kind.   175
Bassanio: I like not fair terms and a villain's mind.
Antonio: Come on: in this there can be no dismay;
My ships come home a month before the day.
                                                  [*Exeunt*]

Act 1, Scene 3: Activities

1. Reread carefully the opening lines of this scene (lines 1-35). Begin a list of descriptive words and phrases which outline your first impressions of Shylock. Note, for example, the careful deliberation of his opening lines, and the extent of his knowledge of Antonio's business. What specific characteristics of Shylock's personality here suggest that he is the antagonist or "villain" of the play?

   First impressions can often be misleading, however. Be prepared to change or add to your list of impressions of Shylock as you learn more about him in this scene and throughout the play.

2. An *aside* is a speech delivered by a character directly to the audience. Although other characters are present on stage, the audience understands that these characters are not supposed to hear the words of the speaker. Thus, an aside allows a character to reveal his innermost thoughts and feelings.

   Reread carefully Shylock's first aside (lines 37-48). Note how our simple view of Shylock as the "villain" becomes more complicated.

   With a partner, rehearse Shylock's speech for reading to the class or recording. Try to project all the different feelings Shylock reveals in his aside.

3. Antonio decides to make an exception to his own rule that he should never borrow money at interest (lines 57-60). Do you think his decision can be justified? Do you admire Antonio for placing more value on friendship than on rules of conduct? Discuss these two questions in a small group.

4. Antonio's speech on "a villain with a smiling cheek" (lines 93-98) is a warning against hypocrisy, that is, a warning

against people who deliberately present false impressions of themselves. Imagine that you are the editor of Shakespeare's text and that this speech has been lost. Knowing what Shakespeare intended, how would you compose Antonio's speech in modern English? Share your version of the speech with a partner. Together, evaluate your success in conveying Antonio's message.

5. What is your reaction to Shylock's account of Antonio's behaviour toward him (lines 102-125)? Imagine yourself in Shylock's position, or in a modern-day situation in which you might be treated in a similar way. Record your feelings in a personal journal entry.

6. a) In the role of a Venetian lawyer, draw up the contract to be signed by Shylock and Antonio. Be sure that the exact terms and conditions are clearly stated.

   b) In the role of the same lawyer, write a letter to a friend in which you express your reaction to this unique contract.

7. Bassanio's final comment in this scene (line 176) uses the device of *foreshadowing*. In other words, his comment hints at events to follow. Using "Predictions" as your title, make a catalogue of all the possible events that might happen in the play. Compare lists with a partner.

8. Debate in parliamentary style: Be it resolved that Bassanio, as he appears in Act 1, is an entirely admirable character. Before you begin, discuss with your teacher the procedure for presenting formal debates.

For the next scene . . .

Why do people gamble? When they gamble, do people ever risk more than money? What role does luck play in gambling? What role does intelligence play in gambling?

Act 2, Scene 1

In this scene . . .

The Prince of Morocco, one of Portia's suitors, has arrived in Belmont. He boasts of his valour and physical courage, but he laments that these outstanding qualities can play no part in a contest controlled by luck. Portia warns the prince that the lottery has a penalty. If he chooses the wrong casket, he will have to swear never to marry.

2   *shadow'd livery:* dark uniform. Liveries are the uniforms worn by footmen, chauffeurs, and other types of servants. Morocco is using a metaphor to describe the colour of his skin. *burnish'd:* shining

3   *near bred:* closely related

4   *fairest:* Is Morocco punning here?

5   *Phoebus' fire:* the sun. Phoebus Apollo was the classical god of the sun.

6   *make incision:* cut ourselves

7   *reddest:* Traditionally, red blood symbolizes courage.

8   *aspect:* appearance, countenance

9   *fear'd:* frightened

10   *best regarded:* most valued, of the highest reputation; *clime:* climate, country

11   *hue:* colour

13-14   *In terms of choice . . . maiden's eyes:* When I choose, I am hard to please, not influenced only by what appeals to my eyes.

15   *the lottery of my destiny:* the contest which controls my future or fate

16   *bars:* denies

17   *scanted:* restricted

18   *hedg'd:* restricted; *wit:* intelligence

18-19   *to yield myself His wife:* to become the wife of the man

20   *stood as fair:* another pun – would have had as fair a chance or would be as attractive to me

24   *scimitar:* short curved sword

25   *Sophy:* Emperor of Persia

26   *Sultan Solyman:* famed commander of the Turkish forces that defeated Persia in 1535

27   *o'erstare:* overstare, outstare

Act 2, Scene 1

Belmont. A room in Portia's house

*Enter the Prince of Morocco, and
his Followers; Portia and Nerissa*

Morocco: Mislike me not for my complexion,
The shadow'd livery of the burnish'd sun,
To whom I am a neighbour, and near bred.
Bring me the fairest creature northward born,
Where Phœbus' fire scarce thaws the icicles,   5
And let us make incision for your love,
To prove whose blood is reddest, his or mine.
I tell thee, lady, this aspect of mine
Hath fear'd the valiant: by my love, I swear
The best regarded virgins of our clime   10
Have lov'd it too: I would not change this hue,
Except to steal your thoughts, my gentle queen.
Portia: In terms of choice I am not solely led
By nice direction of a maiden's eyes;
Besides, the lottery of my destiny   15
Bars me the right of voluntary choosing:
But if my father had not scanted me
And hedg'd me by his wit, to yield myself
His wife who wins me by that means I told you,
Yourself renowned prince, then stood as fair   20
As any corner I have look'd on yet
For my affection.
Morocco: Even for that I thank you:
Therefore, I pray you, lead me to the caskets
To try my fortune. By this scimitar—
That slew the Sophy, and a Persian prince   25
That won three fields of Sultan Solyman—
I would o'erstare the sternest eyes that look;
Outbrave the heart most daring on the earth;
Pluck the young sucking cubs from the she-bear;

32   *Lichas:* a servant of the heroic Hercules

33   *Which is the better man:* to see which is the better man

35   *Alcides:* Hercules, son of Alcaeus; *page:* servant (that is, Lichas)

42   *advis'd:* warned

44   *temple:* probably a small chapel within Portia's palace. There Morocco would take the oath referred to in lines 40-42.

45   *hazard:* chance, risk, gamble

47   *cursed'st:* most cursed

Yea, mock the lion when he roars for prey,   30
To win thee, lady. But, alas the while!
If Hercules and Lichas play at dice
Which is the better man, the greater throw
May turn by fortune from the weaker hand:
So is Alcides beaten by his page;   35
And so may I, blind fortune leading me,
Miss that which one unworthier may attain,
And die with grieving.
Portia: You must take your chance;
And either not attempt to choose at all,
Or swear before you choose, if you choose wrong,   40
Never to speak to lady afterward
In way of marriage: therefore be advis'd.
Morocco: Nor will not: come, bring me unto my chance.
Portia: First, forward to the temple: after dinner
Your hazard shall be made.   45
Morocco: Good fortune then!
To make me blest or cursed'st among men!   [*Exeunt*]

Act 2, Scene 1: Activities

1. What, if anything, does this scene contribute to the plot of the play? Assume you are the director of the play. In your notebook, explore the possible sound and visual effects you might add to this scene to ensure its success.

   You might consider these stage directions which appear in early editions of the play: "Flourish of cornets. Enter Morocco, a tawny Moor all in white, and three or four followers, accordingly, with Portia, Nerissa, and their train."

2. Working in pairs, improvise a radio or television interview with the Prince of Morocco before his meeting with Portia. Find out what he expects Portia's attitude to him will be, especially in view of his nobility and reputation. Ask him why he expects to encounter prejudice in Belmont and how he intends to combat it.

   You could make an audio or video recording of this interview.

3. Contrast Portia's comment to Morocco in lines 20-22 with what she said to Nerissa at the end of Act 1, Scene 2. Would honesty be a better policy? Discuss Portia's behaviour in a small group. Then summarize your own conclusions in a short letter of advice to Portia.

For the next scene . . .

Who are your favourite comedians? How do they make you laugh? What are the skills or techniques of a good comedian?

Act 2, Scene 2

In this scene . . .

Launcelot Gobbo has a dilemma: should he follow
the moral advice of his conscience and stay with his
master Shylock, or should he give in to his temptation
to run away? He has heard that Bassanio is looking
for servants and finally decides not to lose the opportunity for a new position. As he bolts from the stage,
he bumps into his own father, Old Gobbo, who is
so weak in sight that he does not recognize his
son. Launcelot decides to use his father's blindness
to amuse himself and the audience at his father's
expense, but eventually identifies himself. Old Gobbo
has brought a present to Shylock for looking after
his boy; Launcelot insists that the gift be saved for
Bassanio, who now enters.

Bassanio is busy with preparations for his departure to Belmont. There are letters to be written and
delivered, uniforms to be made for his new servants,
torchbearers to be hired for a masquerade, and a
farewell supper to be given for his Venetian friends.
Bassanio is amused by Launcelot's antics and eventually does admit the clown to his service.

As Launcelot goes to take his leave of Shylock,
Gratiano seeks and gains permission to accompany
Bassanio to Belmont – with a promise not to "play the
fool" and ruin Bassanio's chances of success with
Portia.

1 *serve:* assist

2 *fiend:* devil

6 *take heed:* take care and listen

9 *pack:* run away; *Via:* On your way!

10-11 *for the heavens:* for heaven's sake

14 *honest:* good

15-16 *my father . . . kind of taste:* Launcelot hints that his father was not faithful to his wife, but had been intimate with other women.

20 *To be ruled by:* If I were ruled by

22 *God bless the mark:* Pardon me (for what I'm about to say). This self-blessing is a kind of apology to avoid bad luck or evil.

24 *saving your reverence:* begging your pardon. Launcelot is speaking here to the audience, many of whom would have pretended offense at his reference to the devil.

25 *incarnation:* incarnate, in the flesh; *in my conscience:* in my opinion

Scene 2

*Venice. The street outside Shylock's
house*

Enter Launcelot Gobbo

Launcelot: Certainly my conscience will serve me to run from
this Jew my master. The fiend is at mine elbow, and
tempts me, saying to me, 'Gobbo, Launcelot Gobbo,
good Launcelot,' or 'good Gobbo,' or 'good Launcelot
Gobbo, use your legs, take the start, run away.' My   5
conscience says, 'No; take heed, honest Launcelot;
take heed, honest Gobbo;' or, as aforesaid, 'honest
Launcelot Gobbo; do not run; scorn running with thy
heels.' Well, the most courageous fiend bids me pack:
'*Via!*' says the fiend; 'away!' says the fiend; 'for the   10
heavens, rouse up a brave mind,' says the fiend, 'and
run.' Well, my conscience, hanging about the neck of
my heart, says very wisely to me, 'My honest friend
Launcelot, being an honest man's son,'—or rather an
honest woman's son, for, indeed, my father did   15
something smack, something grow to, he had a kind
of taste—well, my conscience says, 'Launcelot, budge
not.' 'Budge!' says the fiend. 'Budge not!' says my
conscience. 'Conscience,' say I, 'you counsel well;'
'Fiend,' say I, 'you counsel well.' To be ruled by my   20
conscience, I should stay with the Jew my master,
who (God bless the mark!) is a kind of devil; and, to
run away from the Jew, I should be ruled by the
fiend, who (saving your reverence) is the devil himself.
Certainly, the Jew is the very devil incarnation; and,   25
in my conscience, my conscience is but a kind of hard
conscience, to offer to counsel me to stay with the
Jew. The fiend gives the more friendly counsel:
I will run, fiend; my heels are at your commandment;
I will run.   30

34   *true-begotten:* fathered. In reality, Launcelot is Gobbo's true-begotten son!

35   *sand-blind:* half-blind; *high gravel-blind:* almost completely blind

36   *try confusions:* try to confuse (by playing tricks on him). However, Launcelot may mean *to try conclusions*, that is, to engage in a battle of wits.

40   *marry:* by the Virgin Mary (in truth)

43   *sonties:* saints; *hit:* find

47   *raise the waters:* make him cry

50   *exceeding:* very

51   *well to live:* in good health

52   *a' :* he

54   *your worship:* The term of respect indicates that Gobbo has still not recognized his son.

55   *ergo:* therefore (Latin). Does Launcelot know the meaning of the word?

57   *an't:* if it

59   *father:* The term was used generally to address an old man, not necessarily one's own father.

61   *the Sisters Three:* the Fates, three godesses in classical mythology who control human destiny

66   *cudgel:* a short stick used as a weapon; *hovel-post:* supporting beam in a poor dwelling

68   *Alack:* alas

Enter Old Gobbo, with a basket

Gobbo: Master young man, you; I pray you, which is the
    way to Master Jew's?

Launcelot: [*Aside*] O heavens! this is my true-begotten father,
    who, being more than sand-blind, high gravel-blind,   35
    knows me not: I will try confusions with him.

Gobbo: Master young gentleman, I pray you, which is the
    way to Master Jew's?

Launcelot: Turn up on your right hand at the next turning,
    but, at the next turning of all, on your left; marry,   40
    at the very next turning, turn of no hand, but turn
    down indirectly to the Jew's house.

Gobbo: By God's sonties, 'twill be a hard way to hit. Can
    you tell me whether one Launcelot, that dwells with
    him, dwell with him or no?   45

Launcelot: Talk you of young Master Launcelot? [*Aside*]
    Mark me now; now will I raise the waters. Talk you
    of young Master Launcelot?

Gobbo: No 'master', sir, but, a poor man's son; his father,
    though I say't, is an honest, exceeding poor man,   50
    and, God be thanked, well to live.

Launcelot: Well, let his father be what 'a will, we talk of
    young Master Launcelot.

Gobbo: Your worship's friend, and Launcelot, sir.

Launcelot: But I pray you, *ergo*, old man, *ergo*, I beseech   55
    you, talk you of young Master Launcelot?

Gobbo: Of Launcelot, an 't please your mastership.

Launcelot: *Ergo*, Master Launcelot. Talk not of Master
    Launcelot, father; for the young gentleman (according
    to fates and destinies and such odd sayings, the sisters   60
    three and such branches of learning) is, indeed,
    deceased; or, as you would say in plain terms, gone
    to heaven.

Gobbo: Marry, God forbid! the boy was the very staff of
    my age, my very prop.   65

Launcelot: [*Aside*] Do I look like a cudgel or a hovel-post,
    a staff or a prop? Do you know me, father?

Gobbo: Alack the day! I know you not, young gentleman:
    but I pray you, tell me, is my boy—God rest his soul!—
    alive or dead?   70

74-75   *it is a wise father . . . child:* in fact, the proverb says, "It is a wise child that knows his own father."

92   *fill-horse:* cart-horse. Many directors have Gobbo stroke the *back* of Launcelot's head during this speech.

97   *agree:* get along

99-100 *set up my rest:* made up my mind

101   *a very Jew:* a true Jew. Notice how Launcelot too reveals the prejudice of Shakespeare's England in its stereotyping of Jews.

102   *halter:* noose (to hang himself)

103   *tell:* count

102-104 *I am famished . . . my ribs:* Rearrange the words to see what Launcelot really means.

106   *liveries:* uniforms

Launcelot: Do you not know me, father?

Gobbo: Alack, sir, I am sand-blind; I know you not.

Launcelot: Nay, indeed, if you had your eyes, you might
    fail of the knowing me: it is a wise father that knows
    his own child. Well, old man, I will tell you news   75
    of your son. [*Kneels*] Give me your blessing: truth will
    come to light; murder cannot be hid long; a man's
    son may, but, in the end, truth will out.

Gobbo: Pray you, sir, stand up. I am sure you are not
    Launcelot, my boy.   80

Launcelot: Pray you, let's have no more fooling about it,
    but give me your blessing: I am Launcelot, your boy
    that was, your son that is, your child that shall be.

Gobbo: I cannot think you are my son.

Launcelot: I know not what I shall think of that; but I am   85
    Launcelot, the Jew's man, and I am sure Margery
    your wife is my mother.

Gobbo: Her name is Margery, indeed: I'll be sworn, if thou
    be Launcelot, thou art mine own flesh and blood.
    Lord worshipped might he be! what a beard hast thou   90
    got! thou hast got more hair on thy chin than Dobbin
    my fill-horse has on his tail.

Launcelot: It should seem then that Dobbin's tail grows
    backward: I am sure he had more hair of his tail than
    I have of my face, when I last saw him.   95

Gobbo: Lord, how art thou changed! How dost thou and
    thy master agree? I have brought him a present. How
    'gree you now?

Launcelot: Well, well: but, for mine own part, as I have set
    up my rest to run away, so I will not rest till I have   100
    run some ground. My master's a very Jew: give him
    a present? give him a halter! I am famished in his
    service; you may tell every finger I have with my ribs.
    Father, I am glad you are come: give me your present
    to one Master Bassanio, who, indeed, gives rare new   105
    liveries. If I serve not him, I will run as far as God
    has any ground. O rare fortune! here comes the man:
    to him, father; for I am a Jew, if I serve the Jew any
    longer.

Enter Bassanio, with Leonardo, and other Servants

110 *You may do so:* Bassanio is already in conversation with Leonardo when he enters; *let it be so hasted that:* hurry so that

112 *put the liveries to making:* arrange for the making of the uniforms

113 *anon:* at once

116 *Gramercy:* Many thanks! (a corruption of the French *grand merci*); *wouldst thou aught:* do you want anything?

120 *infection:* Gobbo means *affection* (desire, wish)

125 *scarce:* hardly; *cater-cousins:* good friends

128 *fruitify:* Launcelot means *specify*, *notify*, or *certify*

131 *impertinent:* Launcelot means *pertinent* (relevant)

137 *defect:* Gobbo means *effect* (point)

138 *suit:* request

140 *preferr'd:* recommended; *preferment:* promotion

143-145 *The old proverb . . . hath 'enough':* The old Scottish proverb is "The grace of God is gear enough," which means that the blessing of God is all one needs (the only *gear* or equipment one needs). Launcelot *parts* or divides the proverb, the first half going to Bassanio and the second half to Shylock.

147-148 *inquire My lodging out:* go to my house

Bassanio: You may do so; but let it be so hasted that supper   110
  be ready at the farthest by five of the clock. See these
  letters delivered; put the liveries to making; and
  desire Gratiano to come anon to my lodging.
                                          [*Exit a Servant*]
Launcelot: To him, father.
Gobbo: God bless your worship!   115
Bassanio: Gramercy! wouldst thou aught with me?
Gobbo: Here's my son, sir, a poor boy—
Launcelot: Not a poor boy, sir, but the rich Jew's man; that
  would, sir—as my father shall specify—
Gobbo: He hath a great infection, sir (as one would say) to   120
  serve—
Launcelot: Indeed, the short and the long is, I serve the
  Jew, and have a desire, as my father shall specify—
Gobbo: His master and he (saving your worship's
  reverence) are scarce cater-cousins.   125
Launcelot: To be brief, the very truth is that the Jew having
  done me wrong, doth cause me—as my father being, I
  hope, an old man, shall frutify unto you—
Gobbo: I have here a dish of doves that I would bestow upon
  your worship, and my suit is—   130
Launcelot: In very brief, the suit is impertinent to myself,
  as your worship shall know by this honest old man;
  and, though I say it, though old man, yet (poor man)
  my father.
Bassanio: One speak for both. What would you?   135
Launcelot: Serve you, sir.
Gobbo: That is the very defect of the matter, sir.
Bassanio: I know thee well; thou hast obtain'd thy suit:
  Shylock thy master spoke with me this day,
  And hath preferr'd thee, if it be preferment   140
  To leave a rich Jew's service, to become
  The follower of so poor a gentleman.
Launcelot: The old proverb is very well parted between my
  master Shylock and you, sir: you have 'the grace of
  God', sir, and he hath 'enough'.   145
Bassanio: Thou speak'st it well. Go, father, with thy son.
  Take leave of thy old master, and inquire
  My lodging out. [*To his Servants*] Give him a livery

149   *guarded:* decorated (with *guards* or bands of colour)

150   *service:* job (as a servant). Launcelot is being sarcastic.

150-151 *I have . . . head:* I have no powers of persuasion.

152   *table:* palm of the hand. In the following lines, Launcelot is pretending to read his palm in order to predict his future.

156   *coming-in:* revenue, income (from their dowries)

157   *'scape:* escape

160   *for this gear:* for giving me this equipment (that is, his new liveries)

161   *in the twinkling:* in an instant (the twinkling of an eye)

163   *bestow'd:* stowed away (in the hold of Bassanio's ship)

164   *feast:* give a feast for

165   *best-esteem'd acquaintance:* favourite friends

166   *herein:* in this matter

170   *suit:* request

173   *rude:* rough, unsophisticated

174   *Parts:* qualities (of character); *become:* fit, suit

177   *liberal:* extravagant

178   *allay:* cool, calm down; *modesty:* moderation

179   *skipping:* boisterous

180   *misconster'd:* miscontrued, misunderstood

More guarded than his fellows': see it done.
Launcelot: Father, in. I cannot get a service, no! I have ne'er 150
  a tongue in my head. Well, [*Looking at his hand*] if
  any man in Italy have a fairer table which doth offer
  to swear upon a book, I shall have good fortune. Go to;
  here's a simple line of life: here's a small trifle of
  wives: alas! fifteen wives is nothing: eleven widows and 155
  nine maids is a simple coming-in for one man; and
  then to 'scape drowning thrice, and to be in peril of
  my life with the edge of a feather-bed; here are simple
  'scapes. Well, if Fortune be a woman, she's a good
  wench for this gear. Father, come; I'll take my leave 160
  of the Jew in the twinkling.
                    [*Exeunt Launcelot* and *Old Gobbo*]
Bassanio: I pray thee, good Leonardo, think on this.
  These things being bought, and orderly bestow'd,
  Return in haste, for I do feast tonight
  My best-esteem'd acquaintance. Hie thee, go. 165
Leonardo: My best endeavours shall be done herein.
  Enter Gratiano
Gratiano: Where's your master?
Leonardo: Yonder, sir, he walks.
                                        [*Exit*]

Gratiano: Signior Bassanio!
Bassanio: Gratiano!
Gratiano: I have a suit to you. 170
Bassanio: You have obtain'd it.
Gratiano: You must not deny me: I must go with you to
  Belmont.
Bassanio: Why, then you must. But here thee, Gratiano;
  Thou art too wild, too rude, and bold of voice—
  Parts that become thee happily enough,
  And in such eyes as ours appear not faults— 175
  But where thou art not known, why, there they show
  Something too liberal. Pray thee, take pain
  To allay with some cold drops of modesty
  Thy skipping spirit, lest, through thy wild behaviour,
  I be misconster'd in the place I go to, 180
  And lose my hopes.
Gratiano: Signior Bassanio, hear me:

182   *sober habit:* a pun: conservative clothing and restrained behaviour

184   *wear:* carry

185   *saying:* being said

188   *Use all . . . civility:* do all the right things at the right time

188   *Like one . . . sad ostent:* like a person well practised in displays of solemnity and seriousness. Gratiano is contradicting the role he outlined earlier in the play.

189   *grandam:* grandmother

190   *bearing:* behaviour

191   *bar:* do not include; *gauge:* judge, measure

If I do not put on a sober habit,
Talk with respect, and swear but now and then,
Wear prayer-books in my pocket, look demurely,
Nay more, while grace is saying, hood mine eyes   185
Thus with my hat, and sigh, and say 'amen',
Use all the observance of civility,
Like one well studied in a sad ostent
To please his grandam, never trust me more.
Bassanio: Well, we shall see your bearing.   190
Gratiano: Nay, but I bar tonight; you shall not gauge me
By what we do tonight.
Bassanio: No, that were pity:
I would entreat you rather to put on
Your boldest suit of mirth, for we have friends
That purpose merriment. But fare you well: 195
I have some business.
Gratiano: And I must to Lorenzo and the rest;
But we will visit you at supper-time.   *[Exeunt]*

Act 2, Scene 2: Activities

1. A soliloquy is a speech in which a character thinks aloud while alone on stage. Launcelot's soliloquy presents his moral dilemma in a comic way. In a group of three, expand the soliloquy. One of you should play Launcelot, one should take the part of his conscience, and one should take the part of temptation. Script your version of the soliloquy for presentation to the class. Be sure to explore methods of conveying humour through both words and actions.

2. With a partner, choose a section of the scene between Launcelot and Old Gobbo and prepare it for dramatic presentation. Emphasize both the verbal humour (puns and nonsense) and the actions that are essential to successful staging of the scene.

3. A *malapropism* is the unintentional and humorous misuse of a word in place of another word which it closely resembles in sound. The term is derived from Mrs. Malaprop, a character in a play written in the eighteenth century, who was constantly using expressions such as "illiterate him" for "obliterate him."

   a) For each of the contemporary examples of malapropism below, select the misused word and determine the word which was intended:
      • Tresspassers will be persecuted!
      • The bullet rickshawed off the wall and hit him in the leg.
      • He finished the race, dripping with inspiration.
      • I like all types of books, but particularly hysterical fiction.

   b) In the role of Launcelot, write a letter to your mother, Margery, in which you tell of your good fortune. Use as many malapropisms as you can. Read your letter to your classmates.

4. With a partner, discuss the ways in which Gratiano's humour is different from Launcelot's. Consider the degree to which each is aware of his own comic effects. Think also about the difference between laughing *at* and laughing *with* a character.

   Remember the comedians you thought of in response to the questions on page 53. Decide whether these comedians are more like Gratiano or Launcelot. Compare your conclusions with those of other groups in the class.

For the next scenes . . .

Why do some teenagers run away from home? What might be some justifiable reasons? How would you counsel a friend who was planning to run away?

Act 2, Scenes 3, 4, 5, and 6

In these scenes . . .

The next four scenes introduce another storyline to the play. Jessica, Shylock's daughter, takes advantage of Launcelot's new position with Bassanio to pass a message to Lorenzo, one of Bassanio's friends and her own secret lover.

Lorenzo, Gratiano, and their friends are planning the entertainment for Bassanio's farewell dinner when Launcelot brings Jessica's letter. Lorenzo reveals to Gratiano the plan of escape which Jessica has devised: the masquerade will provide a perfect opportunity for Jessica, disguised as a page boy, to become Lorenzo's torchbearer and for the lovers to escape together from Venice.

Meanwhile, Shylock learns from Launcelot about the evening's masquerade and orders Jessica to shut herself in the house and pay no attention to the parade in the streets.

Shortly after Shylock's departure, Lorenzo and his friends arrive. Jessica is embarrassed by her male disguise, but is quick to flee with the ducats and jewels she has stolen from her father.

Just as the masquerade is underway, Antonio enters to announce that the winds have changed direction and that Bassanio is setting sail for Belmont without delay.

3   *tediousness:* boredom

10   *Adieu:* Good-bye! *exhibit:* Launcelot means *inhibit* (prevent me from speaking)

11   *pagan:* non-believer (here, a non-Christian)

13   *something:* somewhat

16   *heinous:* horrible, hateful

19   *not to his manners:* not like him in actions

20   *strife:* conflict, struggle

Scene 3

*Venice. The street outside Shylock's
house*

Enter Jessica and Launcelot

Jessica: I am sorry thou wilt leave my father so:
Our house is hell, and thou, a merry devil,
Didst rob it of some taste of tediousness.
But fare thee well; there is a ducat for thee—
And, Launcelot, soon at supper shalt thou see   5
Lorenzo, who is thy new master's guest:
Give him this letter—do it secretly.
And so farewell: I would not have my father
See me in talk with thee.
Launcelot: Adieu! tears exhibit my tongue. Most beautiful   10
pagan, most sweet Jew! If a Christian do not play the
knave and get thee, I am much deceived. But, adieu!
these foolish drops do something drown my manly
spirit: adieu!
Jessica: Farewell, good Launcelot.   *[Exit Launcelot]*   15
Alack, what heinous sin is it in me
To be asham'd to be my father's child!
But though I am a daughter to his blood,
I am not to his manners. O Lorenzo,
If thou keep promise, I shall end this strife,   20
Become a Christian, and thy loving wife.   *[Exit]*

5   *not spoke us yet of:* not yet hired

6   *quaintly order'd:* done in style

9   *furnish us:* get ready

10   *And:* if; *break up:* open (by breaking the seal)

12   *the hand:* the handwriting. Notice the pun on *hand* in line 14.

18   *sup:* dine

22   *masque:* masked ball or masquerade party, preceded by a torch-lit parade through the streets

23   *provided of:* supplied with

Scene 4

Venice. A street.

Enter Gratiano, Lorenzo, Salerio,
and Solanio

Lorenzo: Nay, we will slink away in supper-time,
Disguise us at my lodging, and return
All in an hour.
Gratiano: We have not made good preparation.
Salerio: We have not spoke us yet of torch-bearers.   5
Solanio: 'Tis vile unless it may be quaintly order'd,
And better, in my mind, not undertook.
Lorenzo: 'Tis now but four o'clock: we have two hours
To furnish us.
Enter Launcelot, with a letter
                    Friend Launcelot, what's the news?
Launcelot: And it shall please you to break up this, it shall   10
seem to signify.
Lorenzo: I know the hand: in faith, 'tis a fair hand;
And whiter than the paper it writ on
Is the fair hand that writ.
Gratiano: Love news, in faith.
Launcelot: By your leave, sir.   15
Lorenzo: Whither goest thou?
Launcelot: Marry, sir, to bid my old master, the Jew, to
sup tonight with my new master, the Christian.
Lorenzo: Hold here, take this: tell gentle Jessica
I will not fail her; speak it privately.   20
Go, gentlemen,   [*Exit Launcelot*]
Will you prepare you for this masque tonight?
I am provided of a torch-bearer.
Salerio: Ay, marry, I'll be gone about it straight.
Solanio: And so will I.   25

29   *directed:* instructed

31   *furnish'd:* supplied

32   *page's suit:* costume of a young male servant

35   *foot:* path

36   *she:* misfortune

37   *she is issue to:* Jessica is the child of; *faithless:* unbelieving because he is not a Christian. Of course, Shylock has a faith of his own.

38   *peruse:* look over

Lorenzo: Meet me and Gratiano
  At Gratiano's lodging some hour hence.
Salerio: 'Tis good we do so.
                    [*Exeunt Salerio and Solanio*]
Gratiano: Was not that letter from fair Jessica?
Lorenzo: I must needs tell thee all. She hath directed
  How I shall take her from her father's house;   30
  What gold and jewels she is furnish'd with;
  What page's suit she hath in readiness.
  If e'er the Jew her father come to heaven,
  It will be for his gentle daughter's sake;
  And never dare misfortune cross her foot,   35
  Unless she do it under this excuse,
  That she is issue to a faithless Jew.
  Come, go with me: peruse this as thou goest.
  Fair Jessica shall be my torch-bearer.   [*Exeunt*]

2   *of:* between

3   *What, Jessica:* Shylock calls to his daughter as he speaks with Launcelot. *gormandize:* overeat

5   *rend apparel out:* wear holes in your clothes

7   *bids:* asks

8   *wont:* accustomed, in the habit

12   *wherefore:* why

15   *prodigal:* wasteful

16   *look to:* look after, take care of; *right loath:* very reluctant

17   *rest:* peace of mind

20   *reproach:* What word does Launcelot mean? What is the irony of his malapropism?

22   *conspired:* plotted

22-27   Launcelot may be using another of his nonsensical digressions to conceal his slip of the tongue, commenting upon the use of omens to predict the future. Or he may be mocking Shylock's belief in dreams as omens.

Scene 5

*Venice. The street outside
Shylock's house*

Enter Shylock and Launcelot

Shylock: Well, thou shalt see, thy eyes shall be thy judge
The difference of old Shylock and Bassanio—
What, Jessica!—thou shalt not gormandize
As thou hast done with me—What, Jessica!—
And sleep and snore, and rend apparel out—   5
Why, Jessica, I say!
Launcelot: Why, Jessica!
Shylock: Who bids thee call? I do not bid thee call.
Launcelot: Your worship was wont to tell me that I could
      do nothing without bidding.
      Enter Jessica
Jessica: Call you? What is your will?   10
Shylock: I am bid forth to supper, Jessica;
      There are my keys. But wherefore should I go?
      I am not bid for love: they flatter me.
      But yet I'll go in hate, to feed upon
      The prodigal Christian. Jessica, my girl,   15
      Look to my house. I am right loath to go:
      There is some ill a-brewing towards my rest,
      For I did dream of money-bags tonight.
Launcelot: I beseech you, sir, go: my young master doth
      expect your reproach.   20
Shylock: So do I his.
Launcelot: And they have conspired together—I will not
      say you shall see a masque; but if you do, then it was
      not for nothing that my nose fell a-bleeding on Black
      Monday last, at six o'clock i' the morning, falling out   25
      that year on Ash Wednesday was four year in th'
      afternoon.

30 *wry-neck'd fife:* the fife is a wooden flute which is played side-
ways so that the player must hold his neck and head in a
twisted (*wry*) position

31 *casements:* windows

33 *varnish'd:* wearing painted masks

34 *stop:* block up

35 *shallow foppery:* trivial foolishness

36 *sober:* serious; *By Jacob's staff:* Shylock's oath appropriately
recalls the "success story" of his ancestor Jacob (*Genesis* 32:10).

43 *eye:* look or vigilance

44 *Hagar's offspring:* Ishmael, the illegitimate son of Abraham and
Hagar, the Gentile slave of Abraham's wife (*Genesis* 21). Traditionally, Ishmael represents the outcast.

46 *patch:* clown (who wears patched clothing); *kind:* good, decent

48 *drones:* male bees who do not work

54 *'Fast bind, fast find':* Work out the meaning of this old saying,
remembering that *fast* means tight or secure as well as quick.

56 *if my fortune . . . cross'd:* if I am not unlucky

Shylock: What, are there masques? Here you me, Jessica:
Lock up my doors, and when you hear the drum
And the vile squealing of the wry-neck'd fife,   30
Clamber not you up to the casements then,
Nor thrust your head into the public street
To gaze on Christian fools with varnish'd faces,
But stop my house's ears—I mean my casements—
Let not the sound of shallow foppery enter   35
My sober house. By Jacob's staff I swear
I have no mind of feasting forth tonight;
But I will go. Go you before me, sirrah;
Say I will come.
Launcelot: I will go before, sir. Mistress, look out at window,   40
for all this:

There will come a Christian by,
Will be worth a Jewess' eye.

                                        [*Exit Launcelot*]
Shylock: What says that fool of Hagar's offspring, ha?
Jessica: His words were, 'Farewell, mistress'; nothing else.   45
Shylock: The patch is kind enough, but a huge feeder;
Snail-slow in profit, and he sleeps by day
More than the wild cat: drones hive not with me;
Therefore I part with him, and part with him
To one that I would have him help to waste   50
His borrow'd purse. Well, Jessica, go in—
Perhaps I will return immediately—
Do as I bid you; shut doors after you:
'Fast bind, fast find',
A proverb never stale in thrifty mind.   [*Exit*]   55
Jessica: Farewell; and if my fortune be not cross'd,
I have a father, you a daughter, lost.   [*Exit*]

1   *penthouse:* balcony or second-storey porch

2   *make stand:* wait (for him)

3   *out-dwells his hour:* is late

5   *Venus' pigeons:* The chariot of Venus, Roman goddess of love, was pulled by doves.

5-7   *O ten times . . . unforfeited:* Gratiano and Salerio mock Lorenzo for being late. They suggest that, once a lover has received a commitment, he is no longer as careful or anxious about his behaviour.

11   *unbated:* unabated, equal

14   *a younger or a prodigal:* In the parable, the prodigal son was the younger son (*Luke* 15: 11-32).

15   *scarfed bark:* ship decorated with flags and bunting (perhaps for its maiden voyage)

16   *strumpet:* fickle (in a sexual sense)

8-19   *That ever holds . . . by the strumpet wind:* Gratiano offers three further examples of our habit of beginning something with more enthusiasm than we finish it.

21   *abode:* delay

24   *watch:* stand guard

Scene 6

*Venice. The street outside
Shylock's house*

*Enter Gratiano and Salerio dressed
as masquers*

Gratiano: This is the penthouse under which Lorenzo
   Desir'd us to make stand.
Salerio: His hour is almost past.
Gratiano: And it is marvel he out-dwells his hour,
   For lovers ever run before the clock.
Salerio: O ten times faster Venus' pigeons fly   5
   To seal love's bonds new-made, than they are wont
   To keep obliged faith unforfeited!
Gratiano: That ever holds: who riseth from a feast
   With that keen appetite that he sits down?
   Where is the horse that doth untread again   10
   His tedious measures with the unbated fire
   That he did pace them first? All things that are,
   Are with more spirit chased than enjoy'd.
   How like a younger or a prodigal
   The scarfed bark puts from her native bay,   15
   Hugg'd and embraced by the strumpet wind!
   How like the prodigal doth she return,
   With over-weather'd ribs and ragged sails,
   Lean, rent, and beggar'd by the strumpet wind!
   Enter Lorenzo
Salerio: Here comes Lorenzo: more of this hereafter.   20
Lorenzo: Sweet friends, your patience for my long abode;
   Not I but my affairs have made you wait:
   When you shall please to play the thieves for wives,
   I'll watch as long for you then. Approach;
   Here dwells my father Jew. Ho! who's within?   25

27   *Albeit:* although; *tongue:* voice

33   *casket:* small chest; *pains:* trouble

35   *exchange:* change (of clothing — and sex!)

37   *pretty:* This word has a great many meanings. Here, it probably means *fine* in an ironic sense. Compare the contemporary expression, "A fine mess we're in!"

38   *Cupid:* the Roman god of love, son of Venus, always appearing as an angelic child armed with a bow and arrow

42   *light:* obvious, evident (and also, foolish)

43   *'tis an office of discovery:* torch-bearing is a duty which reveals or lights up

44   *obscur'd:* darkened, hidden. In the next line, Lorenzo takes the meaning as *disguised.*

45   *garnish:* costume

47   *close:* dark and secret; *doth play the runaway:* is passing quickly. Why is the metaphor an appropriate one in this scene?

48   *stay'd:* waited

49   *fast:* secure; *gild:* furnish (literally, decorate with gold)

51   *by my hood:* a mild oath of obscure origin, like "upon my word"; *gentle:* notice again the pun on *Gentile*

52   *Beshrew me:* curse me (another mild oath)

Enter Jessica on the balcony, dressed as a boy
Jessica: Who are you? Tell me, for more certainty,
    Albeit I'll swear that I do know your tongue.
Lorenzo: Lorenzo, and thy love.
Jessica: Lorenzo, certain; and my love indeed,
    For who love I so much? And now who knows   30
    But you, Lorenzo, whether I am yours?
Lorenzo: Heaven and thy thoughts are witness that thou
    art.
Jessica: Here, catch this casket; it is worth the pains.
    I am glad 'tis night, you do not look on me,
    For I am much asham'd of my exchange: 35
    But love is blind, and lovers cannot see
    The pretty follies that themselves commit;
    For if they could, Cupid himself would blush
    To see me thus transformed to a boy.
Lorenzo: Descend, for you must be my torch-bearer.   40
Jessica: What! must I hold a candle to my shames?
    They in themselves, good sooth, are too too light.
    Why, 'tis an office of discovery, love,
    And I should be obscur'd.
Lorenzo: So are you, sweet,
    Even in the lovely garnish of a boy,   45
    But come at once;
    For the close night doth play the runaway,
    And we are stay'd for at Bassanio's feast.
Jessica: I will make fast the doors, and gild myself
    With some more ducats, and be with you straight.   50
                            [Exit above]
Gratiano: Now, by my hood, a gentle, and no Jew.
Lorenzo: Beshrew me, but I love her heartily;
    For she is wise, if I can judge of her;
    And fair she is, if that mine eyes be true;
    And true she is, as she hath prov'd herself;   55
    And therefore, like herself, wise, fair, and true,
    Shall she be placed in my constant soul.
Enter Jessica
    What, art thou come? On, gentlemen; away!
    Our masquing mates by this time for us stay.
                    [Exeunt, except Gratiano]

64   *is come about:* has changed direction

Enter Antonio

Antonio: Who's there?   60

Gratiano: Signior Antonio!

Antonio: Fie, fie, Gratiano! where are all the rest?
 'Tis nine o'clock; our friends all stay for you.
 No masque tonight: the wind is come about;
 Bassanio presently will go aboard: 65
 I have sent twenty out to seek for you.

Gratiano: I am glad on't: I desire no more delight
 Than to be under sail and gone tonight.   *[Exeunt]*

Act 2, Scenes 3, 4, 5, and 6: Activities

1. Make a list of the ways in which the addition of a love affair between Lorenzo and Jessica might complicate the situation for Antonio and Bassanio. Consider *all* the possibilities. Compare your list with that of a partner.

2. In these scenes, our relationship to Shylock becomes more complicated. In a small group, compare and discuss your attitudes to him. How are we led to dislike him *and* to sympathize with him simultaneously? Which emotion predominates in your own reading of these scenes?

   Update the list of descriptive words and phrases that you began in Act 1, and try to reach a group consensus about the nature of Shylock's character to this point in the play.

3. Compare Launcelot's and Shylock's versions of the history of Launcelot's service in Shylock's house. (For Launcelot's side of the story, you will need to review Act 2, Scene 2.)

   If you were directing this play, whose side of the issue would you want the audience to take? Why? In casting the part of Launcelot, how would you help the audience to decide who was telling the truth? Consider obvious physical features as well as Launcelot's attitude, gestures, and voice. Record your ideas in a director's log, and compare notes with others in the class.

4. Make a list of all Bassanio's possible motives for inviting Shylock to dinner. Be sure to find all the clues provided in the text. Which clues might lead you to believe that Bassanio is an "accomplice" in the elopement plot? Why would this evidence be considered merely "circumstantial" in a court of law? As a detective hired by Shylock, write a summary report of your investigation.

5. Debate in parliamentary style: Be it resolved that Shylock shows himself to be a caring and loving father in Scene 5.

6. Discuss with a partner, in a small group, or as a class:

   a) Is Jessica right to elope with Lorenzo?

   b) Is she justified in taking money and jewels with her?

   How do you think Shakespeare's audience would have responded to Jessica's actions? Do you think they would have found irony in Lorenzo's speech praising Jessica (Scene 6, lines 52-57)? Would a modern audience react differently? Why?

7. *Dramatic irony* occurs frequently in Shakespeare's plays. It often springs from the contrast between the knowledge of the audience and the ignorance of a character or characters. In these scenes, there is dramatic irony in Shylock's leaving his house and possessions in Jessica's care. Why?

   In a small group, discuss examples of dramatic irony that you recall from recent television or film viewing. What types of television programs and films appear to provide the richest sources of dramatic irony?

   As a short research project, your group could survey and report on examples of dramatic irony in an average week's television viewing.

For the next scene . . .

What is the possession which you value most? Why do you value it? Is its value obvious to the eye? If not, how would others come to know its importance to you?

Act 2, Scene 7

In this scene . . .

In Belmont, the Prince of Morocco is ready to choose one of the three caskets. He reads aloud the inscription on each one and tries to puzzle out their meanings. As a compliment to Portia, he disregards his belief in his own worth and makes his choice.

1   *discover:* reveal

2   *several:* different

9   *hazard:* venture, risk

12   *I am yours withal:* I and all I own are yours

14   *back again:* in reverse order

19   *fair advantages:* reasonable gains, worthwhile rewards

20   *stoops not . . dross:* does not lower itself to worthless displays. What is a "golden mind"?

21   *aught:* anything

22   *virgin hue:* unblemished sheen or polish

25   *weigh:* consider, estimate; *even:* impartial, unbiased

26   *be'st rated:* be evaluated

Scene 7

Belmont. A room in Portia's house

Enter Portia, with the
Prince of Morocco,
and their Servants

Portia: Go, draw aside the curtains, and discover
The several caskets to this noble prince.
                     [The curtains are drawn back]
Now make your choice.
Morocco: The first, of gold, who this inscription bears:
'Who chooseth me shall gain what many men desire'.   5
The second, silver, which this promise carries:
'Who chooseth me shall get as much as he deserves'.
This third, dull lead, with warning all as blunt:
'Who chooseth me must give and hazard all he hath'.
How shall I know if I do choose the right?   10
Portia: The one of them contains my picture, prince:
If you choose that, then I am yours withal.
Morocco: Some god direct my judgment! Let me see:
I will survey th' inscriptions back again:
What says this leaden casket?   15
'Who chooseth me must give and hazard all he hath'.
Must give! For what? for lead? hazard for lead?
This casket threatens. Men that hazard all
Do it in hope of fair advantages:
A golden mind stoops not to shows of dross;   20
I'll then nor give nor hazard aught for lead.
What says the silver with her virgin hue?
'Who chooseth me shall get as much as he deserves'.
As much as he deserves! Pause there, Morocco,
And weigh thy value with an even hand.   25
If thou be'st rated by thy estimation,

93

29-30   *to be afeard . . . disabling of myself:* to be afraid to choose what I deserve is really to undervalue my worth and to discredit myself

36   *grav'd:* engraved

40   *shrine:* the relics or remains of saints were encased in small caskets or monuments (*shrines*). The saint was often sculpted or painted on the outside of the shrine.

41   *Hyrcanian deserts:* wild uninhabited lands to the south of the Caspian Sea in Asia Minor; *vasty wilds:* vast deserted lands

42   *throughfares:* thoroughfares, highways

44-45   *The watery kingdom . . . face of heaven:* the oceans and seas, whose waves reach up to touch the sky

45   *bar:* obstacle

46   *foreign spirits:* suitors from abroad

47   *As o'er a brook:* as if they had only to cross a stream

49   *Is't like:* is it likely

50-51   *it were too gross . . . obscure grave:* lead would be too vulgar even as a funeral casket to hold (*rib*) her wrapped body in the dark grave. A *cerecloth* is the waxed cloth or shroud in which the body is wrapped.

52   *immur'd:* walled in, contained

53   *tried:* tested (and found to be pure)

54-55   *Never so rich . . . gold:* To what is Morocco comparing Portia in this compliment?

57   *insculpt'd upon:* engraved on the surface of the coin. The "angel" was a gold coin in circulation at this time; it featured the victory of the archangel Michael over a dragon.

60   *thrive:* succeed

61   *form:* likeness, portrait

63   *A carrion Death:* a skull

Thou dost deserve enough; and yet enough
May not extend so far as to the lady:
And yet to be afeard of my deserving
Were but a weak disabling of myself.   30
As much as I deserve! Why, that's the lady:
I do in birth deserve her, and in fortunes,
In graces, and in qualities of breeding;
But more than these, in love I do deserve.
What if I stray'd no further, but chose here?   35
Let's see once more this saying grav'd in gold:
'*Who chooseth me shall gain what many men desire*'.
Why, that's the lady: all the world desires her;
From the four corners of the earth they come,
To kiss this shrine, this mortal breathing saint: 40
The Hyrcanian deserts and the vasty wilds
Of wide Arabia are as throughfares now
For princes to come view fair Portia:
The watery kingdom, whose ambitious head
Spits in the face of heaven, is no bar   45
To stop the foreign spirits, but they come,
As o'er a brook, to see fair Portia.
One of these three contains her heavenly picture.
Is 't like that lead contains her? 'Twere damnation
To think so base a thought: it were too gross   50
To rib her cerecloth in the obscure grave.
Or shall I think in silver she's immur'd,
Being ten times undervalu'd to tried gold?
O sinful thought! Never so rich a gem
Was set in worse than gold. They have in England   55
A coin that bears the figure of an angel
Stamp'd in gold, but that's insculp'd upon;
But here an angel in a golden bed
Lies all within. Deliver me the key:
Here do I choose, and thrive I as I may!   60
Portia: There, take it, prince; and if my form lie there,
    Then I am yours.
                    [*He unlocks the golden casket*]
Morocco: O hell! what have we here?
A carrion Death, within whose empty eye
There is a written scroll. I'll read the writing.

95

65   *glisters:* sparkles, glistens

69   *infold:* contain

71   *What does "old" in judgment mean?*

72   *had not been inscroll'd:* would not have been written on this
      scroll

73   *cold:* dead

77   *tedious:* long, lengthy

79   *complexion:* It seems almost impossible to overlook Portia's
      prejudice here. The word *complexion* can mean personality as
      well as colour (of the skin). Which meaning does Portia intend?
      Or does she intend a pun?

All that glisters is not gold; 65
Often have you heard that told:
Many a man his life hath sold
But my outside to behold:
Gilded tombs do worms infold.
Had you been as wise as bold, 70
Young in limbs, in judgment old,
Your answer had not been inscroll'd.
Fare you well, your suit is cold.

Cold, indeed; and labour lost:
Then farewell heat, and welcome, frost! 75
Portia, adieu. I have too griev'd a heart
To take a tedious leave: thus losers part.

[Exit with his Servants]

Portia:
A gentle riddance. Draw the curtains: go. Let all of his
  complexion choose me so. *[Exeunt]*

Act 2, Scene 7: Activities

1. Using the text, the illustration on page 90, and your own imagination, explain how the spectacle of the room, the three chests, and the costumes suggest the main theme of the scene. Pay particular attention to the message Morocco finds in the gold casket.

   Discuss your thoughts with a partner or small group.

2. As the official scribe (historian) of the court of Morocco, write your account of the Prince's attempt and failure to solve the riddle of the caskets and their inscriptions. Outline the reasoning which led the Prince to his choice.

   As a biased reporter, you could conclude with a defence of your Prince's argument.

   You may wish to prepare and deliver your report in the role of a modern sports commentator.

3. Consider again Morocco's complaint about the lottery, voiced earlier in the play:

   > If Hercules and Lichas play at dice
   > Which is the better man, the greater throw
   > May turn by fortune from the weaker hand . . .
   > (Scene 1, lines 31-33)

   With a partner or in a small group, assess the validity of Morocco's comparison of the lottery to a game of chance. How might Portia's father have defended his lottery against this accusation? How, then, is the casket lottery *not* a "lottery" in the usual sense?

4. "All that glisters is not gold."
   Write a short fable to illustrate the truth of this moral. You might want to adopt the style of Aesop by using animal characters, or you might use a more realistic and con-temporary style.

For the next scene . . .

Why do people sometimes laugh at the misfortune of others? How do comedians take advantage of this human tendency to make an audience laugh? Have you ever felt uncomfortable about sharing this sense of humour? Why or why not?

Act 2, Scene 8

In this scene . . .

Back in Venice, Salerio and Solanio discuss the whereabouts of Lorenzo. Shylock, as might be expected, has assumed that Bassanio conspired with Lorenzo and Jessica to help them escape to Belmont. However, Antonio has sworn that the lovers did not sail with Bassanio. Solanio entertains Salerio with an impersonation of the outraged Shylock. Salerio then describes the tearful parting of Antonio and Bassanio the previous evening, and expresses the fear that Antonio may well suffer the consequences of Shylock's fury against his daughter.

4   *rais'd:* roused (from sleep)

7   *given to understand:* told

10   *certified:* assured, convinced

12   *passion:* emotional outburst

13   *outrageous:* excessive, uncontrolled

25   *look he keep his day:* be careful to make his repayment on the appointed day

26   *well remember'd:* a good point to keep in mind

27   *reason'd:* talked

29   *miscarried:* perished, was lost

30   *richly fraught:* carrying rich cargo

Scene 8

Venice. A street

Enter Salerio and Solanio

Salerio: Why, man, I saw Bassanio under sail,
  With him is Gratiano gone along;
  And in their ship I am sure Lorenzo is not.
Solanio: The villain Jew with outcries rais'd the duke,
  Who went with him to search Bassanio's ship.   5
Salerio: He came too late, the ship was under sail,
  But there the duke was given to understand
  That in a gondola were seen together
  Lorenzo and his amorous Jessica.
  Besides, Antonio certified the duke   10
  They were not with Bassanio in his ship.
Solanio: I never heard a passion so confus'd,
  So strange, outrageous, and so variable,
  As the dog Jew did utter in the streets:
  'My daughter! O my ducats! O my daughter!   15
  Fled with a Christian! O my Christian ducats!
  Justice! the law! my ducats, and my daughter!
  A sealed bag, two sealed bags of ducats,
  Of double ducats, stol'n from me by my daughter!
  And jewels! two stones, two rich and precious stones,   20
  Stol'n by my daughter! Justice! find the girl!
  She hath the stones upon her, and the ducats.'
Salerio: Why, all the boys in Venice follow him,
  Crying his stones, his daughter, and his ducats.
Solanio: Let good Antonio look he keep his day,   25
  Or he shall pay for this.
Salerio: Marry, well remember'd.
  I reason'd with a Frenchman yesterday,
  Who told me, in the narrow seas that part
  The French and English, there miscarried
  A vessel of our country richly fraught.   30

35   *treads:* walks

39   *Slubber not business:* do not rush and be careless about your
        business

40   *the very riping of the time:* until the right moment

44   *ostents:* expressions, demonstrations

45   *As shall . . . there:* as will create a good impression of you in
        Belmont

48   *wondrous sensible:* amazingly tender

50   *he only loves . . . for him:* Antonio cares about the world only
        because he loves Bassanio

52   *quicken:* enliven, make more active, cheerful, give life to; *his
        embraced heaviness:* the seriousness which he has adopted

I thought upon Antonio when he told me,
And wish'd in silence that it were not his.
Solanio: You were best to tell Antonio what you hear;
Yet do not suddenly, for it may grieve him.
Salerio: A kinder gentleman treads not the earth.   35
I saw Bassanio and Antonio part:
Bassanio told him he would make some speed
Of his return: he answer'd, 'Do not so;
Slubber not business for my sake, Bassanio,
But stay the very riping of the time;   40
And for the Jew's bond which he hath of me,
Let it not enter in your mind of love:
Be merry, and employ your chiefest thoughts
To courtship and such fair ostents of love
As shall conveniently become you there.'   45
And even there, his eye being big with tears,
Turning his face, he put his hand behind him,
And with affection wondrous sensible
He wrung Bassanio's hand; and so they parted.
Solanio: I think he only loves the world for him.   50
I pray thee, let us go and find him out,
And quicken his embraced heaviness
With some delight or other.
Salerio: Do we so.
                                             [*Exeunt*]

Act 2, Scene 8: Activities

1. How do you respond to Solanio's description of Shylock's reactions to the elopement (lines 12-22)? Record your response in your journal, taking the following questions into consideration: How does the impersonation increase or lessen your sympathy for Shylock? How does it affect your attitude toward Solanio and his friends? How comfortable do you feel about sharing Solanio's humour?

2. Do you agree with Solanio that Shylock will try to punish Antonio for Jessica's elopement? Why would he do so? Compose the entry Shylock might write in his diary upon returning from his humiliating parade through the streets. What connections does he make between the loss of his daughter and his agreement with Antonio?

   Be sure to include all the events, from Shylock's leaving for dinner with Bassanio to his return home for the night.

3. The fact that Shylock knows his daughter has eloped with Lorenzo suggests that Jessica might have left him a letter. Compose the letter that you think Jessica would have left.

4. *Melodrama* is a form of theatre in which emotional scenes and speeches are dramatized in a heightened or exaggerated style. Television soap operas, particularly their "tear-jerking" scenes, provide the best contemporary examples. Salerio's description of Bassanio and Antonio at the end of this scene might be considered melodramatic.

   With a partner, improvise and script a new dialogue between Antonio and Bassanio, avoiding melodrama but capturing the spirit of their friendship. Be prepared to present your scripts to the class.

ə . . .
_____

Jge your own work? Why is it
ʳ try to judge your own merit as a
ʲief danger in attempting this?

Act 2, Scene 9

In this scene . . .

In Belmont, Portia has a new suitor, the Prince of Arragon. Portia reminds him that, if he chooses to try the casket lottery and fails, he will have to abide by three promises. Arragon surveys the inscriptions on the caskets. Scornful of popular taste and filled with self-love, Arragon makes his choice. Just as he is reading the scroll he finds inside the casket, news arrives that Bassanio has reached Belmont.

2   *ta'en:* taken

3   *election:* selection, choice

6   *nuptial rites be solemnized:* marriage ceremony be performed

9   *enjoin'd:* committed, bound

10   *unfold:* reveal

11-12 *fail Of the right casket:* fail to choose correctly

16   *injunctions:* commands, restrictions

21   *You:* Arragon addresses the leaden casket directly; *ere:* before

25   *Multitude:* the masses, common or ordinary people; *show:* outward appearance

26   *fond:* foolish

27   *pries not:* does not pry (look) into; *like the martlet:* The martlet is a bird which builds its nest on the outward walls of buildings, thus exposing its nest to the dangers of unpredictable weather.

Scene 9

Belmont. A room in Portia's house

Enter Nerissa, with a Servant

Nerissa: Quick, quick, I pray thee; draw the curtain straight:
The Prince of Arragon hath ta'en his oath,
And comes to his election presently.
            [*Curtains drawn to reveal caskets*]
Enter the Prince of Arragon, Portia, and Servants
Portia: Behold, there stand the caskets, noble prince:
If you choose that wherein I am contain'd,   5
Straight shall our nuptial rites be solemniz'd;
But if you fail, without more speech, my lord,
You must be gone from hence immediately.
Arragon: I am enjoin'd by oath to observe three things:
First, never to unfold to any one   10
Which casket 'twas I chose; next, if I fail
Of the right casket, never in my life
To woo a maid in way of marriage; lastly,
If I do fail in fortune of my choice,
Immediately to leave you and be gone.   15
Portia: To these injunctions every one doth swear
That comes to hazard for my worthless self.
Arragon: And so have I address'd me. Fortune now
To my heart's hope! Gold, silver, and base lead.
'*Who chooseth me must give and hazard all he hath.*'   20
You shall look fairer, ere I give or hazard.
What says the golden chest? ha! let me see:
'*Who chooseth me shall gain what many men desire*'.
What many men desire! that 'many' may be meant
By the fool multitude, that choose by show,   25
Not learning more than the fond eye doth teach,
Which pries not to th' interior, but, like the martlet,
Builds in the weather on the outward wall,
Even in the force and road of casualty.

31   *jump with:* go along with

32   *rank me with:* join (the ranks of); *barbarous:* coarse, unrefined

37   *cozen:* cheat

37-38   *be honourable . . . merit:* gain reputation (*honour*) without deserving it

40   *estates, degrees, and offices:* possessions, social rank, and positions

41   *deriv'd:* gained; *clear:* unsullied, pure, bright

42   *purchas'd:* won

43   *cover:* wear a hat. In Shakespearean times, the lower classes were expected to bare their heads in the presence of the aristocracy.

45   *glean'd:* culled, picked out

46   *seed of honour:* children of the nobility

47   *chaff and ruin of the times:* the poorest and lowest of people

45-48   Arragon implies that many of the nobility deserve to be peasants. Conversely, some peasants deserve to be aristocrats.

50   *desert:* that I deserve

53   *portrait:* depiction (not necessarily a painting)

54   *schedule:* scroll

60   *To offend . . . offices:* those who commit an offence may not be their own judges

62   *The fire . . . tried this:* Silver is refined (*tried*) in a furnace seven times to guarantee its purity.

63-64   *Seven times . . . choose amiss:* A person's judgment must be as refined as pure silver to avoid choosing wrongly (*amiss*).

I will not choose what many men desire,   30
Because I will not jump with common spirits
And rank me with the barbarous multitudes.
Why, then to thee, thou silver treasure-house;
Tell me once more what title thou dost bear:
'*Who chooseth me shall get as much as he deserves*'.   35
And well said too; for who shall go about
To cozen fortune, and be honourable
Without the stamp of merit? Let none presume
To wear an undeserved dignity.
O that estates, degrees, and offices   40
Were not deriv'd corruptly, and that clear honour
Where purchas'd by the merit of the wearer.
How many then should cover that stand bare!
How many be commanded that command!
How much low peasantry would then be glean'd   45
From the true seed of honour! and how much honour
Pick'd from the chaff and ruin of the times
To be new varnish'd! Well, but to my choice:
'*Who chooseth me shall get as much as he deserves*'.
I will assume desert. Give me a key for this,   50
And instantly unlock my fortunes here.
                          [*He opens the silver casket*]
Portia: Too long a pause for that which you find there.
Arragon: What's here? the portrait of a blinking idiot,
Presenting me a schedule! I will read it.
How much unlike art thou to Portia!   55
How much unlike my hopes and my deservings!
'*Who chooseth me shall have as much as he deserves*'.
Did I deserve no more than a fool's head?
Is that my prize? are my deserts no better?
Portia: To offend, and judge, are distinct offices,   60
And of opposed natures.
Arragon: What is here?

    The fire seven times tried this:
    Seven times tried that judgment is
    That did never choose amiss
    Some there be that shadows kiss: 65
    Such have but a shadow's bliss.

67   *iwis:* indeed, certainly

68   *silver'd o'er:* covered with silver (so that the foolishness is hidden). The scroll makes reference to old men whose silver hair makes them appear wise.

71   *sped:* finished

78   *sing'd:* burned

79   *deliberate fools:* fools who deliberate (reason) too much

81   *no heresy:* true, not a false belief

82   Put Nerissa's proverb into your own words.

85   *alighted:* dismounted (from his horse)

86   *before:* in advance

87   *signify:* announce

88   *sensible regreets:* tangible greetings (in the form of gifts)

89   *to wit:* that is to say; *commends:* compliments; *breath:* words, speech

90   *Yet:* until now

91   *likely:* fitting

93   *costly:* rich, bountiful

94   *fore-spurrer:* messenger, herald

96   *anon:* soon; *kin:* relation

97   *high-day:* high-flown, extravagant

99   *post:* messenger; *mannerly:* with such courtesy

100   *lord Love:* Cupid, the young god of love

There be fools alive, iwis,
Silver'd o'er; and so was this.
Take what wife you will to bed,
I will ever be your head.   70
So be gone: you are sped.

Still more fool I shall appear
By the time I linger here:
With one fool's head I came to woo,
But I go away with two.   75
Sweet, adieu. I'll keep my oath,
Patiently to bear my wrath.
                              [*Exit Arragon with his Servants*]
Portia: Thus hath the candle sing'd the moth.
   O these deliberate fools! when they do choose,
   They have the wisdom by their wit to lose.   80
Nerissa: The ancient saying is no heresy:
   'Hanging and wiving goes by destiny.'
Portia: Come, draw the curtain, Nerissa.
   Enter a Servant
Servant: Where is my lady?
Portia: Here; what would my lord?
Servant: Madam, there is alighted at your gate   85
   A young Venetian, one that comes before
   To signify th' approaching of his lord;
   From whom he bringeth sensible regreets,
   To wit, besides commends and courteous breath,
   Gifts of rich value. Yet I have not seen   90
   So likely an ambassador of love.
   A day in April never came so sweet
   To show how costly summer was at hand,
   As this fore-spurrer comes before his lord.
Portia: No more, I pray thee: I am half afeard   95
   Thou wilt say anon he is some kin to thee,
   Thou spend'st such high-day wit in praising him.
   Come, come, Nerissa; for I long to see
   Quick Cupid's post that comes so mannerly.
Nerissa: Bassanio, lord Love, if thy will it be!   [*Exeunt*] 100

Act 2, Scene 9: Activities

1. In pairs or small groups, discuss whether Arragon's reasoning in this scene is different from that of Morocco in Act 2, Scene 7. Given Portia's father's intention that the lottery be a test of character, which of the two princes proves more worthy? Why?

2. With a partner, improvise and script a dialogue between Morocco and Arragon in which each defends his choice of casket to the other. Share your dialogue with other pairs.

3. You now know which casket contains the portrait of Portia. From what you have learned about Bassanio, do you think he will choose correctly? Why or why not? Discuss this question in a small group, using the list of Bassanio's characteristics which you began to compile after the first scene of the play.

4. Imagine that you are Shakespeare. The members of your acting troupe, the King's Men, have argued that this scene should be eliminated because the audience is already certain from Morocco's choice that Portia's portrait is in the leaden casket.

   Prepare and deliver to the class the speech in which you justify including this scene. Your speech should select and develop at least one of the scene's many dramatic, thematic, and comedic possibilities.

For the next scene . . .

"Revenge is sweet!" Recall a situation in which you seriously contemplated taking revenge on someone. Why did you want revenge? How did you plan to seek revenge? What finally determined your decision to put your plan into action or to abandon it?

Act 3, Scene 1

In this scene . . .

The action of the play returns to Venice where the bond between Antonio and Shylock is almost due. Salerio has heard bad news about one of Antonio's ships, but he is quick to realize that Shylock's determination to revenge Jessica's elopement is a far greater threat to his friend. When Shylock enters, Salerio asks him outright what possible use a pound of human flesh could be. Shylock's famous answer contains not only an eloquent defence of his own humanity, but also a clear indication that nothing will distract him from full revenge upon his enemies. Tubal enters with upsetting news of Jessica and the way she has been wasting the money and jewels she stole. He soothes Shylock with a prediction of Antonio's bankruptcy.

2   *yet it lives:* there is a persistent rumour; *unchecked:* undenied

3   *lading:* cargo; *the narrow seas:* the English Channel (between England and France)

4   *the Goodwins:* the Goodwin Sands, a sandbar in the middle of the Channel

5   *flat:* sandbar

6   *my gossip Report:* the old woman who is my informer (Report or Rumour is personified here)

8   *I would:* I wish; *that:* her report

9   *knapped:* chewed, nibbled; *ginger:* Ginger was commonly associated with old people in Elizabethan times. It may have been a digestive aid.

11   *prolixity:* long-windedness

15   *Come, the full stop:* Come to your point!

19   *betimes:* immediately. Solanio wants to conclude Salerio's prayer with the formal *amen* (so be it) before it can be foiled by the devil; *cross:* thwart. Note the pun. Some Christians make the sign of the cross when they have finished a prayer. The devil, of course, would never bless or answer a prayer, but frustrate (*cross*) its intentions.

26   *withal:* with

28   *fledge:* fledged, ready to fly (with new feathers on its young wings); *complexion:* nature, disposition

29   *dam:* mother

31   *the devil:* Salerio means Shylock. Note his earlier comparison in line 20.

Act 3, Scene 1

Venice. A street

Enter Solanio and Salerio

Solanio: Now, what news on the Rialto?
Salerio: Why, yet it lives there unchecked that Antonio hath
a ship of rich lading wrecked on the narrow seas—
the Goodwins, I think they call the place, a very
dangerous flat, and fatal, where the carcasses of many   5
a tall ship lie buried, as they say, if my gossip Report
be an honest woman of her word.
Solanio: I would she were as lying a gossip in that as ever
knapped ginger, or made her neighbours believe she
wept for the death of a third husband. But it is true—   10
without any slips of prolixity or crossing the plain
highway of talk—that the good Antonio, the honest
Antonio—O, that I had a title good enough to keep his
name company!
Salerio: Come, the full stop.   15
Solanio: Ha! what say'st thou? Why, the end is, he hath
lost a ship.
Salerio: I would it might prove the end of his losses.
Solanio: Let me say 'amen' betimes, lest the devil cross my
prayer, for here he comes, in the likeness of a Jew.   20
Enter Shylock
How now, Shylock! what news among the merchants?
Shylock: You knew, none so well, none so well as you, of
my daughter's flight.
Salerio: That's certain: I, for my part, knew the tailor that   25
made the wings she flew withal.
Solanio: And Shylock, for his own part, knew the bird was
fledge; and then it is the complexion of them all to
leave the dam.
Shylock: She is damned for it.   30
Salerio: That's certain, if the devil may be her judge.
Shylock: My own flesh and blood to rebel!

33   *Out upon it:* curse it (your body); *old carrion:* old man (with a tired and decaying body); *rebels it at these years:* do you still feel lust at your age? Solanio pretends that Shylock is referring to the rebellion of his own body against his mind and insults him by suggesting that he no longer has control over his sexual urges. Shylock clarifies his meaning in the next line.

36   *jet:* a black mineral

37   *Rhenish:* white wine from the Rhine Valley in Germany

40   *match:* bargain

42   *that was used to:* who used to; *smug:* neatly and richly dressed

43   *mart:* marketplace; *look to:* pay attention to (both "look after" and "be careful of")

44   *wont:* accustomed; *usurer:* "loan shark"

45   *for a Christian courtesy:* as a favour. Charity (love for one's fellow human being) is considered the greatest of Christian virtues.

49   *To bait fish withal:* to use as bait for fishing

51   *hindered me:* prevented me (from earning a profit)

53   *bargains:* business deals; *cooled . . . heated:* What does Shylock mean here?

55   *dimensions:* bodily size and shape

64   *what is his humility:* what happens to the humbleness or meekness which the New Testament commands (*Matthew* 5: 39-44)? Shylock answers his own question in a single word, *Revenge!*

65   *what should his sufferance be:* how should he endure it? Shylock is prepared to disregard this Jewish virtue ("For sufferance is the badge of all our tribe" Act 1, Scene 3, line 106) as readily as the Christian disregards his humility.

67-68   *it shall go hard but . . . the instruction:* no matter what happens I will be even more vengeful than you have taught me to be

Solanio: Out upon it, old carrion! rebels it at these years?
Shylock: I say my daughter is my flesh and my blood.
Salerio: There is more difference between thy flesh and hers   35
  than between jet and ivory; more between your bloods
  than there is between red wine and Rhenish. But tell
  us, do you hear whether Antonio have had any loss
  at sea or no?
Shylock: There I have another bad match: a bankrupt, a   40
  prodigal, who dare scarce show his head on the Rialto;
  a beggar, that was used to come so smug upon the
  mart. Let him look to his bond! he was wont to call
  me usurer. Let him look to his bond! he was wont
  to lend money for a Christian courtesy. Let him look   45
  to his bond!
Salerio: Why, I am sure, if he forfeit thou wilt not take his
  flesh: what's that good for?
Shylock: To bait fish withal: if it will feed nothing else, it
  will feed my revenge. He hath disgraced me, and   50
  hindered me half a million, laughed at my losses,
  mocked at my gains, scorned my nation, thwarted my
  bargains, cooled my friends, heated mine enemies; and
  what's his reason? I am a Jew. Hath not a Jew eyes?
  hath not a Jew hands, organs, dimensions, senses,   55
  affections, passions? fed with the same food, hurt
  with the same weapons, subject to the same diseases,
  healed by the same means, warmed and cooled by
  the same winter and summer, as a Christian is? If you
  prick us, do we not bleed? if you tickle us, do we not   60
  laugh? if you poison us, do we not die? and if you
  wrong us, shall we not revenge? If we are like you in
  the rest, we will resemble you in that. If a Jew wrong
  a Christian, what is his humility? Revenge! If a
  Christian wrong a Jew, what should his sufferance be   65
  by Christian example? Why, revenge! The villainy
  you teach me I will execute, and it shall go hard but I
  will better the instruction.
  Enter a Servant
Servant: Gentlemen, my master Antonio is at his house,
  and desires to speak with you both.   70
Salerio: We have been up and down to seek him.

73-74   *a third cannot be matched:* these two cannot be matched by a third

79   *Frankfurt:* In medieval times, an international fair was held in Frankfurt, Germany, twice each year.

80-81   *I never felt it till now:* Shylock discounts the history of the persecution and suffering of his people in comparison with his own misery.

84   *hearsed:* laid out in her coffin

89   *but what lights o':* except what alights on, lands on

89-90   *but o' my breathing:* except the ones that I breathe

94   *cast away:* wrecked

101   *fourscore:* eighty (a score is twenty)

103   *at a sitting:* on a single occasion, at one time

105   *divers:* several

107   *break:* go broke, declare bankruptcy

Enter Tubal

Solanio: Here comes another of the tribe: a third cannot be
matched, unless the devil himself turn Jew.

[*Exeunt Solanio, Salerio and Servant*]

Shylock: How now, Tubal! what news from Genoa? Hast   75
thou found my daughter?

Tubal: I often came where I did hear of her, but cannot
find her.

Shylock: Why there, there, there, there! a diamond gone,
cost me two thousand ducats in Frankfurt! The curse
never fell upon our nation till now; I never felt it   80
till now: two thousand ducats in that, and other
precious, precious jewels. I would my daughter were
dead at my foot, and the jewels in her ear! would she
were hearsed at my foot, and the ducats in her coffin!
No news of them—why so? and I know not what's   85
spent in the search. Why thou—loss upon loss! the thief
gone with so much, and so much to find the thief;
and no satisfaction, no revenge: nor no ill luck stirring
but what lights o' my shoulders; no sighs but o' my
breathing; no tears but o' my shedding.   90

Tubal: Yes, other men have ill luck too. Antonio, as I heard
in Genoa—

Shylock: What, what, what? ill luck? ill luck?

Tubal: —hath an argosy cast away, coming from Tripolis.

Shylock: I thank God! I thank God! Is it true? is it true?   95

Tubal: I spoke with some of the sailors that escaped the
wreck.

Shylock: I thank thee, good Tubal. Good news, good news!
ha, ha! Heard in Genoa?

Tubal: Your daughter spent in Genoa, as I heard, one night,   100
fourscore ducats.

Shylock: Thou stick'st a dagger in me: I shall never see my
gold again: fourscore ducats at a sitting! fourscore
ducats!

Tubal: There came divers of Antonio's creditors in my   105
company in Venice, that swear he cannot choose but
break.

Shylock: I am very glad of it: I'll plague him; I'll torture
him: I am glad of it.

110   *of:* from

112   *Out upon her:* Curse her! Damn her!

113   *I had it of Leah:* it was a gift from Leah

116-117 *fee me an officer:* hire an officer (to arrest Antonio)

117   *bespeak him a fortnight before:* order him to be ready two weeks before the bond falls due

118-119 *were he out . . . I will:* if he were gone from Venice, I would be able to conduct my business unhindered and unchecked

Tubal: One of them showed me a ring that he had of your   110
daughter for a monkey.
Shylock: Out upon her! Thou torturest me, Tubal: it was
my turquoise; I had it of Leah when I was a bachelor:
I would not have given it for a wilderness of monkeys.
Tubal: But Antonio is certainly undone.   115
Shylock: Nay, that's true, that's very true. Go, Tubal, fee
me an officer; bespeak him a fortnight before. I will
have the heart of him, if he forfeit; for, were he out
of Venice, I can make what merchandise I will. Go,
Tubal, and meet me at our synagogue; go, good   120
Tubal; at our synagogue, Tubal.
                    [*Exeunt in different directions*]

Act 3, Scene 1: Activities

1. Solanio and Salerio's mockery brings Shylock to an emotional outburst in which he "justifies" revenge (lines 49-69).

   a) In a small group, read the speech aloud several times so that you can fully appreciate Shylock's words. Then trace the logical steps in Shylock's argument.

   b) Decide what your group considers to be the strongest and the weakest point of Shylock's argument, and report your findings to the class. Do different groups have different interpretations?

2. In this scene, Tubal returns from his mission to locate Jessica in Genoa. With a partner, improvise or script the "missing" scene in which Shylock sends Tubal to Genoa to search for his missing daughter and money. As playwrights, consider these questions:
   - What is Shylock's state of mind as he issues Tubal his instructions?
   - What are his purposes and priorities in sending Tubal to Genoa?
   - What is Tubal to do if and when he finds Jessica?
   - What is Tubal's attitude toward his assignment?

   Compare your scenes with those of other pairs. Note and discuss differences in interpretation, especially of Shylock's character.

3. This is the only scene in which Tubal appears. With a partner, discuss the purpose of his appearance.

   Rehearse and present your version of his conversation with Shylock to the class, or tape it in an audio or video recording. Consider the following questions when playing the part of Tubal:
   - Is he old or young?
   - Is he clever or slow?
   - Is he comic or serious?
   - Is he sympathetic or indifferent to Shylock's feelings?

Be sure to think about the way in which Tubal's personality and attitude may affect the audience's perception of Shylock.

4. "I would not have given in for a wilderness of monkeys!" Shylock's reaction to the thoughtless sale of his precious memento of Leah (*presumably* his wife, now dead) reveals that he can be tender and sentimental. Write a letter from the *young* Shylock to Leah that shows this aspect of his character. Establish a specific context for the letter: a time, a place, and an occasion. You might consider a letter of thanks for the ring, a first love letter, a formal proposal of marriage, or a letter from overseas.

For the next scene . . .

"Rules are meant to be broken." Do you agree with this old saying? Are there any rules which should never be broken? What are they? Are there any rules which could be broken without loss of integrity? Under what conditions might the breaking of rules be justified?

Act 3, Scene 2

In this scene . . .

In Belmont, Portia and Bassanio have fallen in love, and all thoughts of time and obligation have passed from Bassanio's mind. Bassanio is eager, however, to have Portia as his wife and is anxious to make his casket choice. Portia begs him to wait a few days longer, but Bassanio cannot bear the torture of further delay. After contemplating the difference between appearance and reality, he chooses the lead casket and wins Portia as his wife. Gratiano adds to the mood of celebration with news of his own marriage plans, and an exchange of rings and promises brings the scene to a climax of happiness and joy.

However, the mood alters after Lorenzo and Jessica arrive unexpectedly with Salerio, who has brought a letter for Bassanio from Venice. Antonio has written to announce that all of his ships have been lost. Three months have passed since his bond with Shylock was signed and he is now completely within Shylock's power.

1   *tarry:* wait

2   *hazard:* take a risk

3   *forbear:* hold back

5   *I would not:* I do not want to

6   *Hate counsels . . . quality:* hatred does not give this kind of advice

10   *venture:* take a risk

11   *I am forsworn:* I would be breaking my promise (for her promise, see Act 1, Scene 2, lines 105-107)

12   *so:* in this situation (that is, forsworn); *miss:* lose

14   *Beshrew:* shame on

15   *o'erlooked:* cast a spell upon, bewitched

20   *Prove it so:* if it should prove so, if it turns out this way

22   *peise:* slow down

23   *eke it . . . out:* make it last

24   *To stay you from election:* to delay you from making your choice

25   *rack:* an instrument of torture which stretched the victim's body over a wooden frame. The rack was commonly used to force confessions from suspected traitors and heretics.

29   *fear th'enjoying of my love:* be afraid that I shall never have the one I love

Scene 2

Belmont. A room in Portia's house

Enter Bassanio, Portia, Gratiano,
Nerissa, and Servants

Portia: I pray you, tarry, pause a day or two
  Before you hazard; for, in choosing wrong,
  I lose your company: therefore, forbear awhile.
  There's something tells me (but it is not love)
  I would not lose you; and you know yourself,   5
  Hate counsels not in such a quality.
  But lest you should not understand me well—
  And yet a maiden hath no tongue but thought—
  I would detain you here some month or two
  Before you venture for me. I could teach you   10
  How to choose right, but then I am forsworn;
  So will I never be: so may you miss me—
  But if you do, you'll make me wish a sin,
  That I had been forsworn. Beshrew your eyes,
  They have o'erlook'd me and divided me: 15
  One half of me is yours, the other half yours—
  Mine own, I would say; but if mine, then yours,
  And so all yours. O these naughty times
  Put bars between the owners and their rights;
  And so, though yours, not yours. Prove it so,   20
  Let fortune go to hell for it, not I.
  I speak too long; but 'tis to peise the time,
  To eke it and to draw it out in length,
  To stay you from election.
Bassanio: Let me choose;
  For as I am, I live upon the rack.   25
Portia: Upon the rack, Bassanio! then confess
  What treason there is mingled with your love.
Bassanio: None but that ugly treason of mistrust,
  Which makes me fear th' enjoying of my love:

30-31   *There may as well . . . my love:* There is as little friendship (*amity*) between snow and fire as there is between treason and my love

33   *enforced:* forced (by the pain of the torture)

36   *Had been . . . confession:* is all I have to confess

38   *deliverance:* release

42   *aloof:* aside, to the side

44   *a swan-like end:* Swans do not sing. However, the Elizabethans believed that a swan did sing a beautiful lament immediately before its death.

46   *May stand more proper:* may be complete. Work out the full meaning of Portia's metaphor.

49   *flourish:* fanfare

51   *dulcet:* sweet

54   *presence:* dignity, nobility

55   *Alcides:* Hercules, who was the son of Alcaeus. Hercules rescued the Trojan princess Hesione, who had been offered by her father as a sacrifice to the sea-monster that was threatening to destroy Troy.

58   *Dardanian:* Trojan (descended from Dardanus, the legendary founder of Troy)

59   *bleared visages:* tear-stained faces

60   *issue:* outcome

61   *Live thou:* if you live

62   *fray:* fight

63   *fancy:* infatuation, shallow love, love based upon physical attraction

65   *begot:* begun

There may as well be amity and life   30
'Tween snow and fire, as treason and my love.
Portia: Ay, but I fear you speak upon the rack,
  Where men enforced do speak anything.
Bassanio: Promise me life, and I'll confess the truth.
Portia: Well, then, confess, and live.   35
Bassanio: 'Confess and love'
  Had been the very sum of my confession:
  O happy torment, when my torturer
  Doth teach me answers for deliverance!
  But let me to my fortune and the caskets.
Portia: Away then! I am lock'd in one of them: 40
  If you do love me, you will find me out.
  Nerissa and the rest, stand all aloof.
  Let music sound while he doth make his choice;
  Then, if he lose, he makes a swan-like end,
  Fading in music: that the comparison   45
  May stand more proper, my eye shall be the stream
  And watery death-bed for him. He may win;
  And what is music then? then music is
  Even as the flourish when true subjects bow
  To a new-crowned monarch: such it is   50
  As are those dulcet sounds in break of day
  That creep into the dreaming bridegroom's ear,
  And summon him to marriage. Now he goes,
  With no less presence, but with much more love,
  Than young Alcides, when he did redeem   55
  The virgin tribute paid by howling Troy
  To the sea-monster: I stand for sacrifice;
  The rest aloof are the Dardanian wives,
  With bleared visages come forth to view
  The issue of th' exploit. Go, Hercules!   60
  Live thou, I live: with much, much more dismay
  I view the fight than thou that mak'st the fray.
  [*A Song whilst Bassanio comments on the caskets to himself.*]

> *Tell me where is fancy bred,*
> *Or in the heart or in the head?*
> *How begot, how nourished?*   65
> *Reply, reply.*

67   *engend'red:* born, begotten

70   *knell:* funeral bell

73   *least themselves:* not in the least what they appear to be

74   *The world:* people; *still:* continually, forever; *ornament:* outward appearance

75-77   *In law . . . show of evil:* in a court, a legal argument, however faulty and dishonest, may sound convincing when it is disguised by a brilliant speaker.

78   *damned error:* false belief; *sober brow:* seemingly honest and educated person

79   *text:* a passage from the Bible (compare this with Antonio's remark in Act 1, Scene 3, line 94)

81-82   *There is no vice . . . outward parts:* all vices may be disguised by an outward show of virtue.

85   *beards:* Beards were considered to be a sign of manliness and courage. *Mars:* the classical god of war

86   *livers white as milk:* The liver of a brave man would be red with blood (compare with Morocco's boast in Act 2, Scene 1, line 7).

87   *valour's excrement:* the outward show (beards) of courage

88   *To render them redoubted:* to make them look frightening

88-89   *Look on beauty . . . weight:* In Elizabethan times, cosmetics were sold by weight.

91   *lightest:* both "lightest in colour" (therefore, fairest, most beautiful) and "lightest in morality" (least pure, least innocent)

92-95   *So are those . . . second head:* In Elizabethan times, wigs were made with hair cut from corpses.

97   *guiled:* full of guile or deceit

99   *Indian beauty:* dark beauty would have been a contradiction in terms for Shakespeare's audience.

102   *Hard food for Midas:* According to Greek legend, the ancient king of Phrygia in Asia Minor was so greedy that he wished that all he touched might become gold. Once his wish came true, he almost starved to death.

103   *common drudge:* lowly servant (*common* because silver passes from hand to hand as coins)

104   *meagre:* poor, undecorated

105   *aught:* anything

It is engend'red in the eyes,
With gazing fed; and fancy dies
In the cradle where it lies.
    Let us all ring fancy's knell: 70
    I'll begin it—Ding, dong, bell.
    Ding, dong, bell.

Bassanio: So may the outward shows be least themselves:
The world is still deceiv'd with ornament.
In law, what plea so tainted and corrupt 75
But, being season'd with a gracious voice,
Obscures the show of evil? In religion,
What damned error, but some sober brow
Will bless it and approve it with a text,
Hiding the grossness with fair ornament? 80
There is no vice so simple but assumes
Some mark of virtue on his outward parts.
How many cowards, whose hearts are all as false
As stairs of sand, wear yet upon their chins
The beards of Hercules and frowning Mars, 85
Who, inward search'd, have livers white as milk;
And these assume but valour's excrement
To render them redoubted. Look on beauty,
And you shall see 'tis purchas'd by the weight;
Which therein works a miracle in nature, 90
Making them lightest that wear most of it:
So are those crisped snaky golden locks
Which make such wanton gambols with the wind,
Upon supposed fairness, often known
To be the dowry of a second head, 95
The skull that bred them in the sepulchre.
Thus ornament is but the guiled shore
To a more dangerous sea, the beauteous scarf
Veiling an Indian beauty; in a word,
The seeming truth which cunning times put on 100
To entrap the wisest. Therefore, thou gaudy gold,
Hard food for Midas, I will none of thee;
Nor none of thee, thou pale and common drudge
'Tween man and man: but thou, thou meagre lead,
Which rather threaten'st than dost promise aught, 105

107   *consequence:* result, outcome

108   *fleet to:* vanish into

109   *As:* such as; *rash-embrac'd:* too quickly accepted

110   *green-eyed jealousy:* Compare the expression *green with envy.*

111   *allay:* restrain

112   *measure:* moderation; *scant:* restrain

114   *surfeit:* suffer from having too much

115   *counterfeit:* likeness, portrait

115-116 *What demi-god . . . creation:* What artist was so divine that he was able to paint a picture so remarkably life-like?

116   *Move these eyes:* Do these eyes move?

117   *riding . . . mine:* controlled by my own gazing

118   *sever'd:* parted

119-120 *so sweet a bar . . . sweet friends:* it is appropriate that such sweet breath should part such sweet lips

120-123 *Here in her hairs . . . gnats in cobwebs:* Bassanio compares Portia's hair to a spider's web. Do you find this metaphor either appropriate or flattering?

125   *it:* the one eye which he has already painted

126   *unfurnish'd:* unpartnered (by a second eye)

126-129 *Yet look . . . substance:* Just as my praise cannot adequately describe the beauty of this portrait, so the portrait does not capture the beauty of Portia herself.

130   *continent:* container

140   *by note:* according to the instructions (found in lines 137-138)

141   *contending in a prize:* competing in a contest (fencing, wrestling, archery, or some other sport)

Thy paleness moves me more than eloquence,
And here choose I: joy be the consequence!
Portia: [*Aside*] How all the other passions fleet to air,
As doubtful thoughts, and rash-embrac'd despair,
And shuddering fear, and green-eyed jealousy.   110
O love be moderate, allay thy ecstasy,
In measure rain thy joy, scant this excess,
I feel too much thy blessing; make it less,
For fear I surfeit!
Bassanio: What find I here?
                    [*He opens the leaden casket*]
Fair Portia's counterfeit! What demi-god   115
Hath come so near creation? Move these eyes?
Or whether, riding on the balls of mine,
Seem they in motion? Here are sever'd lips,
Parted with sugar breath; so sweet a bar
Should sunder such sweet friends. Here in her hairs   120
The painter plays the spider, and hath woven
A golden mesh t'entrap the hearts of men
Faster than gnats in cobwebs: but her eyes!
How could he see to do them? having made one,
Methinks it should have power to steal both his   125
And leave itself unfurnish'd: yet look how far
The substance of my praise doth wrong this shadow
In underprizing it, so far this shadow
Doth limp behind the substance. Here's the scroll,
The continent and summary of my fortune.   130

> *You that choose not by the view,*
> *Chance as fair, and choose as true!*
> *Since this fortune falls to you,*
> *Be content and seek no new.*
> *If you be well pleas'd with this*   135
> *And hold your fortune for your bliss,*
> *Turn you where your lady is*
> *And claim her with a loving kiss.*

A gentle scroll. Fair lady, by your leave;
                              [*Kissing her*]
I come by note, to give and to receive.   140
Like one of two contending in a prize,

143   *universal shout:* shouts of support from everyone

144   *in a doubt:* uncertain, unsure

145   *his or no:* for him or not

148   *ratified:* formally guaranteed (that is, with the kiss promised by the scroll)

153   *trebled:* tripled

155   *That only to:* only so that I may; *account:* estimation, opinion

156   *livings:* material possessions

157   *Exceed account:* be worth more than you can estimate

158   *to term in gross:* to put it bluntly or to state in full

159   *unpractis'd:* inexperienced

160   *Happy:* fortunate, lucky (as well as *happy* in the modern sense)

162   *is not bred so dull:* was not born so stupid

167   *but now:* just a moment ago

173   *presage the ruin:* signify or represent the end

174   *vantage to exclaim on you:* opportunity to reproach you

175   *bereft me:* taken from me

176   *Only my blood . . . veins:* Only my blushing tells you what I feel

177-183 *And there is . . . not express'd:* Bassanio compares himself to a crowd which is overcome with joy as it responds to a rousing speech by its beloved prince.

That thinks he hath done well in people's eyes,
Hearing applause and universal shout,
Giddy in spirit, still gazing in a doubt
Whether those peals of praise be his or no;   145
So, thrice-fair lady, stand I, even so,
As doubtful whether what I see be true,
Until confirm'd, sign'd, ratified by you.
Portia: You see me, Lord Bassanio, where I stand,
    Such as I am: though for myself alone   150
    I would not be ambitious in my wish,
    To wish myself much better; yet, for you,
    I would be trebled twenty times myself;
    A thousand times more fair, ten thousand times
        more rich;
    That only to stand high in your account,   155
    I might in virtues, beauties, livings, friends,
    Exceed account: but the full sum of me
    Is sum of something, which, to term in gross,
    Is an unlesson'd girl, unschool'd, unpractis'd;
    Happy in this, she is not yet so old   160
    But she may learn; happier than this,
    She is not bred so dull but she can learn;
    Happiest of all, is that her gentle spirit
    Commits itself to yours to be directed
    As from her lord, her governor, her king.   165
    Myself and what is mine, to you and yours
    Is now converted: but now I was the lord
    Of this fair mansion, master of my servants,
    Queen o'er myself; and even now, but now,
    This house, these servants, and this same myself   170
    Are yours, my lord's. I give them with this ring;
    Which when you part from, lose, or give away,
    Let it presage the ruin of your love,
    And be my vantage to exclaim on you.
Bassanio: Madam, you have bereft me of all words,   175
    Only my blood speaks to you in my veins;
    And there is such confusion in my powers,
    As, after some oration fairly spoke
    By a beloved prince, there doth appear
    Among the buzzing pleased multitude;   180

187   *prosper:* come true

192   *your honours:* form of address to show respect for superiors; *solemnize:* make legal (in a marriage ceremony)

193   *bargain:* contract

195   *so:* provided that

199-200 *for intermission . . . than you:* I haven't been wasting my time any more than you have been

201   *stood:* depended

203   *until I sweat again:* so hard that I began to sweat

204   *swearing:* making promises and oaths of love; *roof:* the roof (top) of his mouth

213   *play with them:* place bets with them

215   *stake down:* put our money on the table now. In the following line, Gratiano responds with a bawdy pun.

217   *infidel:* non-Christian

Where every something, being blent together,
Turns to a wild of nothing, save of joy,
Express'd, and not express'd. But when this ring
Parts from this finger, then parts life from hence:
O then be bold to say Bassanio's dead.   185
Nerissa: My lord and lady, it is now our time,
   That have stood by and seen our wishes prosper,
   To cry, good joy. Good joy, my lord and lady!
Gratiano: My Lord Bassanio, and my gentle lady,
   I wish you all the joy that you can wish;   190
   For I am sure you can wish none from me.
   And when your honours mean to solemnize
   The bargain of your faith, I do beseech you,
   Even at that time I may be married too.
Bassanio: With all my heart, so thou canst get a wife.   195
Gratiano: I thank your lordship, you have got me one.
   My eyes, my lord, can look as swift as yours:
   You saw the mistress, I beheld the maid;
   You lov'd, I lov'd: for intermission
   No more pertains to me, my lord, than you.   200
   Your fortune stood upon the caskets there,
   And so did mine too, as the matter falls;
   For wooing here until I sweat again,
   And swearing till my very roof was dry
   With oaths of love, at last (if promise last)   205
   I got a promise of this fair one here
   To have her love, provided that your fortune
   Achiev'd her mistress.
Portia: Is this true, Nerissa?
Nerissa: Madam, it is, so you stand pleas'd withal.
Bassanio: And do you, Gratiano, mean good faith?   210
Gratiano: Yes, faith, my lord.
Bassanio: Our feast shall be much honour'd in your marriage.
Gratiano: We'll play with them the first boy for a thousand
   ducats.
Nerissa: What, and stake down?   215
Gratiano: No, we shall ne'er win at that sport and stake
   down!
   But who comes here? Lorenzo and his infidel!
   What! and my old Venetian friend, Salerio?

220-221 *If that the youth . . . welcome:* if I have the right to welcome you, considering that my authority here is so recent

222 *very:* true

231 *Commends him:* sends his greetings; *Ere I ope:* before I open

235 *estate:* both "state of mind" and "financial situation"

236 *yond stranger:* the stranger over there

238 *royal:* both "worthy" and "wealthy"

240 *We are the Jasons:* See Bassanio's earlier allusion to the golden fleece in Act 1, Scene 1, line 170.

242 *shrewd:* hurtful

245 *constitution:* temperament (as revealed by the changing colour of Bassanio's complexion)

246 *constant:* even-tempered

247 *With leave:* excuse me

251 *blotted:* stained (with ink)

Enter Lorenzo, Jessica, and Salerio
Bassanio: Lorenzo, and Salerio, welcome hither,
    If that the youth of my new interest here   220
    Have power to bid you welcome. By your leave,
    I bid my very friends and countrymen,
    Sweet Portia, welcome.
Portia: So do I, my lord:
    They are entirely welcome.
Lorenzo: I thank your honour. For my part, my lord,   225
    My purpose was not to have seen you here,
    But meeting with Salerio by the way,
    He did entreat me, past all saying nay,
    To come with him along.
Salerio: I did, my lord,
    And I have reason for it. Signior Antonio   230
    Commends him to you.   *[Gives Bassanio a letter]*
Bassanio: Ere I ope his letter,
    I pray you, tell me how my good friend doth.
Salerio: Not sick, my lord, unless it be in mind;
    Nor well, unless in mind: his letter there
    Will show you his estate.   235
                [Bassanio opens the letter]
Gratiano: Nerissa, cheer yond stranger; bid her welcome.
    Your hand, Salerio. What's the news from Venice?
    How doth that royal merchant, good Antonio?
    I know he will be glad of our success;
    We are the Jasons, we have won the fleece.   240
Salerio: I would you had won the fleece that he hath lost.
Portia: There are some shrewd contents in yond same
        paper,
    That steals the colour from Bassanio's cheek:
    Some dear friend dead, else nothing in the world
    Could turn so much the constitution   245
    Of any constant man. What, worse and worse!
    With leave, Bassanio; I am half yourself,
    And I must freely have the half of anything
    That this same paper brings you.
Bassanio: O sweet Portia! 250
    Here are a few of the unpleasant'st words
    That ever blotted paper. Gentle lady,

252   *impart:* confess

256   *Rating:* valuing

257   *braggart:* boaster

258   *state:* estate, fortune

260   *engag'd:* committed, bound, indebted

261   *mere:* absolute

262   *To feed my means:* to supply myself with money

266   *hit:* success

273   *present money:* ready cash; *discharge:* pay off his debt to

274   *He:* Shylock

275   *keen:* both "eager" and "cruel"; *confound:* destroy, ruin

276   *plies:* begs, urges

277   *impeach the freedom of the state:* cast doubt upon the reputation
        of Venice as a city of justice and equality

279   *magnificoes:* Venetian senators and noblemen

280   *port:* power, authority, social rank; *persuaded with him:* tried to
        persuade him

281   *envious plea:* malicious demand

282   *forfeiture:* penalty

288   *deny not:* do not prevent him

When I did first impart my love to you,
I freely told you all the wealth I had
Ran in my veins—I was a gentleman—
And then I told you true; and yet, dear lady,   255
Rating myself at nothing, you shall see
How much I was a braggart. When I told you
My state was nothing, I should then have told you
That I was worse than nothing; for, indeed,
I have engag'd myself to a dear friend,   260
Engag'd my friend to his mere enemy,
To feed my means. Here is a letter, lady;
The paper as the body of my friend,
And every word in it a gaping wound,
Issuing life-blood. But is it true, Salerio?   265
Hath all his ventures fail'd? What, not one hit?
From Tripolis, from Mexico, and England,
From Lisbon, Barbary, and India?
And not one vessel 'scape the dreadful touch
Of merchant-marring rocks?   270
Salerio: Not one, my lord.
Besides, it should appear, that if he had
The present money to discharge the Jew,
He would not take it. Never did I know
A creature, that did bear the shape of man,   275
So keen and greedy to confound a man.
He plies the duke at morning and at night,
And doth impeach the freedom of the state,
If they deny him justice: twenty merchants,
The duke himself, and the magnificoes
Of greatest port, have all persuaded with him;   280
But none can drive him from the envious plea
Of forfeiture, of justice, and his bond.
Jessica: When I was with him, I have heard him swear
To Tubal and to Chus, his countrymen,
That he would rather have Antonio's flesh   285
Than twenty times the value of the sum
That he did owe him; and I know, my lord,
If law, authority, and power deny not,
It will go hard with poor Antonio.
Portia: Is it your dear friend that is thus in trouble?   290

292   *best-conditioned:* most able, most ready

293   *courtesies:* acts of kindness

294   *ancient Roman honour:* loyalty to friends and country

298   *deface:* cancel

309   *maids:* unmarried women

310   *shall hence:* shall go from here

312   *dear:* expensive; *Since you are . . . dear:* What is Portia's pun?

316   *forfeit:* overdue, past due

319   *use your pleasure:* do as you wish

321   *dispatch:* hurry to complete

324-325   *No bed . . . twain:* I shall not sleep, or even rest, until we are together again

Bassanio: The dearest friend to me, the kindest man,
    The best-condition'd and unwearied spirit
    In doing courtesies, and one in whom
    The ancient Roman honour more appears
    Than any that draws breath in Italy.   295
Portia: What sum owes he the Jew?
Bassanio: For me, three thousand ducats.
Portia: What, no more?
    Pay him six thousand, and deface the bond;
    Double six thousand, and then treble that,
    Before a friend of this description   300
    Shall lose a hair through Bassanio's fault.
    First go with me to church and call me wife,
    And then away to Venice to your friend;
    For never shall you lie by Portia's side
    With an unquiet soul. You shall have gold   305
    To pay the petty debt twenty times over:
    When it is paid, bring your true friend along.
    My maid Nerissa and myself meantime
    Will live as maids and widows. Come, away!
    For you shall hence upon your wedding-day.   310
    Bid your friends welcome, show a merry cheer;
    Since you are dear bought, I will love you dear.
    But let me hear the letter of your friend.
Bassanio: Sweet Bassanio, my ships have all miscarried, my
    creditors grow cruel, my estate is very low, my bond to the 315
    Jew is forfeit; and since, in paying it, it is impossible I
    should live, all debts are cleared between you and I, if I
    might but see you at my death. Notwithstanding, use your
    pleasure; if your love do not persuade you to come, let not
    my letter.   320
Portia: O love, dispatch all business, and be gone!
Bassanio: Since I have your good leave to go away,
    I will make haste; but, till I come again,
    No bed shall e'er be guilty of my stay,
    Nor rest be interposer 'twixt us twain.   *[Exeunt]* 325

Act 3, Scene 2: Activities

1. The audience already knows, before the scene begins, that Portia's picture is in the leaden casket. As a director, you would have to decide whether this fact decreases the suspense in the first half of the scene. In your director's log, record the instructions you would you give to the actors playing Portia and Bassanio to heighten the level of suspense for your audience. Consider positioning and movement of the actors on stage, variations in vocal rhythm and inflection, pauses in the action, and the use of facial expression and gesture.

2. How does Portia's first speech in the scene (lines 1-24) show us a side of her character we have not seen before? Is the Portia we see here consistent with the Portia we have seen in earlier scenes? How do you react to her at this point? Share your observations with a partner or in a small group.

3. Reread carefully the song in lines 63-72. Do you think it contains direct clues to the correct casket? Do you think that Portia has betrayed her promise to her father by calling for this song?

   a) In pairs, improvise or script a scene in which Portia justifies breaking the rules of the casket lottery to Nerissa. Be sure to include Nerissa's responses, real- izing that she, too, has an interest in Bassanio's success.

   b) As William Shakespeare, write a letter directed against critics who have charged that the inclusion of the song makes your romantic hero and heroine less than admirable people.

   c) As a director, decide whether you would include or cut the song in a full-scale production of the play. Outline the reasons for your decision in a director's log.

4. Do you consider the long speech in which Bassanio justifies his choice of the lead casket (lines 73-107) to reflect a character consistent with the Bassanio we know? Consult the list of Bassanio's characteristics which you have been compiling. If Bassanio missed the clues in the song, how might you account for his newfound wisdom? If you believe he has understood the clues, why do you think he takes so long to make his choice?

   In a small group, discuss your responses to these three questions. Work toward a consensus on Bassanio's worthiness as Portia's victorious suitor.

   Record your own thoughts in a personal journal entry.

5. Debate in parliamentary style: Be it resolved that, in lines 149-174, Portia describes the ideal relationship between a woman and her husband.

6. In this scene, Shakespeare interweaves three main storylines or plots of his play: the casket plot, the bond plot, and the elopement plot. With a partner, devise a diagram or chart in which you show how these three plots connect with one another in this scene.

7. You are the Duke of Venice. Shylock has been "plying you at morning and at night" to uphold his case against Antonio. You are in a dilemma, for you know that victory *or* defeat for Shylock will reflect badly upon the state of Venice. As the Duke, write a letter to your friend, a noted lawyer, briefly outlining the situation, expressing your fears and requesting practical advice.

For the next scene . . .

Have you ever tried to reason with someone who was overcome with emotion? Why is this such a difficult task? What are the chances of success? What advice would you give if a friend were trying to reason with someone who was very upset?

Act 3, Scene 3

In this scene . . .

In accordance with Shylock's arrangements, Antonio
has been arrested and taken to debtor's prison. His
jailer will have to produce the prisoner when the court
calls for him. In the meantime, he has gone out walking
with Antonio. They meet Shylock who is angry that
Antonio has any freedom whatsoever and berates
the jailer for allowing Antonio in the street. Antonio
attempts to reason with Shylock, but he cannot moderate Shylock's vindictive hatred. Solanio cannot believe
that the Duke will uphold Shylock's claim to a pound
of Antonio's flesh. However, Antonio knows that the
Duke cannot cancel the bond without damaging
Venice's reputation as a just state in which the rights
of all traders are protected.

1   *look to him:* guard him carefully

9   *naughty:* worthless, wicked; *fond:* foolish
10   *abroad:* outside, in the streets (that is, away from the prison)

14   *dull-eyed:* stupid

16   *intercessors:* go-betweens, pleaders

18   *impenetrable cur:* insensitive and unfeeling dog
19   *kept with:* lived among
20   *bootless:* useless

22   *deliver'd:* rescued; *forfeitures:* legal suits against debtors
23   *made moan:* cried for help

25   *grant this forfeiture to hold:* allow this suit to be upheld in court

Scene 3

Venice. A street

Enter Shylock, Solanio, Antonio,
and Gaoler

Shylock: Gaoler, look to him: tell not me of mercy;
  This is the fool that lent out money gratis:
  Gaoler, look to him.
Antonio: Hear me yet, good Shylock.
Shylock: I'll have my bond; speak not against my bond:
  I have sworn an oath that I will have my bond.   5
  Thou call'dst me dog before thou hadst a cause,
  But, since I am a dog, beware my fangs:
  The duke shall grant me justice. I do wonder,
  Thou naughty gaoler, that thou art so fond
  To come abroad with him at his request.   10
Antonio: I pray thee, hear me speak.
Shylock: I'll have my bond; I will not hear thee speak:
  I'll have my bond, and therefore speak no more.
  I'll not be made a soft and dull-eyed fool,
  To shake the head, relent, and sigh, and yield   15
  To Christian intercessors. Follow not;
  I'll have no speaking; I will have my bond.   *[Exit]*
Solanio: It is the most impenetrable cur
  That ever kept with men.
Antonio: Let him alone:
  I'll follow him no more with bootless prayers.   20
  He seeks my life; his reason well I know.
  I oft deliver'd from his forfeitures
  Many that have at times made moan to me;
  Therefore he hates me.
Solanio: I am sure the duke
  Will never grant this forfeiture to hold.   25

27   *commodity:* rights, privileges; *strangers:* foreigners, non-Venetians (including Jews). Venice was known for the personal freedom allowed to non-citizens within its borders.

29   *impeach:* discredit, cast doubt upon

31   *Consisteth of all nations:* Venice depended upon international trade for its wealth and power.

32   *bated:* reduced (in weight)

34   *bloody:* bloodthirsty

Antonio: The duke cannot deny the course of law:
For the commodity that strangers have
With us in Venice, if it be denied,
Will much impeach the justice of the state,
Since that the trade and profit of the city   30
Consisteth of all nations. Therefore, go:
These griefs and losses have so bated me,
That I shall hardly spare a pound of flesh
Tomorrow to my bloody creditor.
Well, gaoler, on. Pray God, Bassanio come   35
To see me pay his debt, and then I care not!   [*Exeunt*]

Act 3, Scene 3: Activities

1. Antonio thinks he knows why Shylock wants to destroy him (lines 22-25). Do you think the reason Antonio gives is enough to account for Shylock's malice? As the audience, what do you know about Shylock's motives that Antonio does not take into account?

   a) Make notes on your own conclusions to these questions. Be sure to review Shylock's earlier scenes in order to find the evidence which supports your conclusions.

   b) In a small group, use your notes to draw up a list of Shylock's principal motives for pursuing revenge on Antonio. Rank these motives in order of importance to Shylock. All members of your group must agree on the order of importance. This will require careful consideration and assessment of everyone's point of view.

   Present your list of motives for comparison and discussion with the whole class.

2. If you were directing a production of the play, would you keep this short scene, or leave it out? Explain the reasons for your decision in a director's log.

3. In a small group, rewrite this short scene in modern English and present it to the class live or on videotape. Retain the original setting and situation, but feel free to experiment with details, images, and language.

For the next scenes . . .

"Any friend of yours is a friend of mine." What is the meaning of this traditional saying? What obligations does it place upon friendship?

Act 3, Scenes 4 and 5

In these scenes . . .

Portia asks Lorenzo to look after her estate, telling him that she and Nerissa are retreating to a nunnery to pray for their husbands' safe return. In reality, they plan to follow Bassanio and Gratiano to Venice, disguised as men.

When Portia and Nerissa have gone, Launcelot, who has travelled to Belmont with his new master, teases Jessica about her unavoidable damnation to hell. Lorenzo joins in the fun, claiming that, as his wife, Jessica will at least experience the "joys of heaven here on earth."

2   *conceit:* understanding

3   *amity:* friendship

7   *lover:* close friend

8-9 *you would be . . . enforce you:* you would be more proud of this special act of kindness than of your usual acts of common courtesy and charity

12   *waste:* pass, spend

13   *Whose souls . . . love:* who share a friendship to which each is equally committed. Pairs of working oxen are linked together by a double collar made of wood and called a *yoke.*

14   *needs:* of necessity

15   *lineaments:* physical features or characteristics

17   *bosom lover:* best friend

19   *bestow'd:* spent

20   *the semblance of my soul:* Antonio (her soul itself would be Bassanio)

25   *husbandry and manage:* careful management

Scene 4

Belmont. A room in Portia's house

Enter Portia, Nerissa, Lorenzo,
Jessica and Balthazar

Lorenzo: Madam, although I speak it in your presence,
    You have a noble and a true conceit
    Of god-like amity; which appears most strongly
    In bearing thus the absence of your lord.
    But if you knew to whom you show this honour,   5
    How true a gentleman you send relief,
    How dear a lover of my lord your husband,
    I know you would be prouder of the work
    Than customary bounty can enforce you.
Portia: I never did repent for doing good,   10
    Nor shall not now: for in companions
    That do converse and waste the time together,
    Whose souls do bear an equal yoke of love,
    There must be needs a like proportion
    Of lineaments, of manners, and of spirit;   15
    Which makes me think that this Antonio,
    Being the bosom lover of my lord,
    Must needs be like my lord, If it be so,
    How little is the cost I have bestow'd
    In purchasing the semblance of my soul   20
    From out the state of hellish cruelty!
    This comes too near the praising of myself;
    Therefore, no more of it: hear other things.
    Lorenzo, I commit into your hands
    The husbandry and manage of my house   25
    Until my lord's return: for mine own part,
    I have toward heaven breath'd a secret vow
    To live in prayer and contemplation,
    Only attended by Nerissa here,
    Until her husband and my lord's return.   30

33   *imposition:* request

37   *My people:* my household servants

46   *ever:* always

49   *render:* give

50   *Doctor:* In Shakespeare's time, this title was applied to all of the professions. Doctor Bellario is, in fact, a lawyer, not a physician. At this time, the University of Padua enjoyed international fame as a centre of learning.

52   *with imagin'd speed:* as quickly as may be imagined

53   *traject:* wharf, dock. The medieval Italian word for a ferry is *traghetto.*

54   *trades:* travels back and forth

56   *all convenient speed:* as fast as I can

57   *in hand:* to be done

60   *habit:* costume

61   *accomplished:* equipped

62   *With that we lack:* with what we do not have

63   *accoutered:* dressed

66   *between the change . . . boy:* as if my voice were breaking

67   *reed:* squeaky; *mincing:* dainty

There is a monastery two miles off,
And there we will abide. I do desire you
Not to deny this imposition,
The which my love and some necessity
Now lays upon you.   35
Lorenzo: Madam, with all my heart:
I shall obey you in all fair commands.
Portia: My people do already know my mind,
And will acknowledge you and Jessica
In place of Lord Bassanio and myself.
So fare you well till we shall meet again.   40
Lorenzo: Fair thoughts and happy hours attend on you!
Jessica: I wish your ladyship all heart's content.
Portia: I thank you for your wish, and am well pleas'd
To wish it back on you: fare you well, Jessica.
                              [*Exeunt Jessica and Lorenzo*]
Now, Balthazar,   45
As I have ever found thee honest-true,
So let me find thee still. Take this same letter,
And use thou all th' endeavour of a man
In speed to Padua: see thou render this
Into my cousin's hand, Doctor Bellario;   50
And look what notes and garments he doth give thee,
Bring them, I pray thee, with imagin'd speed
Unto the traject, to the common ferry
Which trades to Venice. Waste no time in words,
But get thee gone: I shall be there before thee.   55
Balthazar: Madam, I go with all convenient speed.   [*Exit*]
Portia: Come on, Nerissa: I have work in hand
That you yet know not of: we'll see our husbands
Before they think of us.
Nerissa: Shall they see us?
Portia: They shall, Nerissa; but in such a habit   60
That they shall think we are accomplished
With that we lack. I'll hold thee any wager,
When we are both accoutered like young men,
I'll prove the prettier fellow of the two,
And wear my dagger with the braver grace,   65
And speak between the change of man and boy
With a reed voice, and turn two mincing steps

68 *frays:* fights, quarrels

69 *quaint:* ingenious, elaborate

72 *I could not do withal:* I could do nothing to help it

74 *puny:* feeble

77 *raw:* youthful, crude; *bragging Jacks:* boastful men

78 *turn to men:* turn ourselves into men. Portia pretends to take the meaning differently.

80 *lewd:* dirty-minded

81 *device:* plan

Into a manly stride, and speak of frays
Like a fine bragging youth, and tell quaint lies,
How honourable ladies sought my love,   70
Which I denying, they fell sick and died—
I could not do withal; then I'll repent,
And wish, for all that, that I had not kill'd them.
And twenty of these puny lies I'll tell,
That men shall swear I have discontinu'd school   75
Above a twelvemonth. I have within my mind
A thousand raw tricks of these bragging Jacks,
Which I will practise.
Nerissa: Why, shall we turn to men?
Portia: Fie, what a question's that,
If thou wert near a lewd interpreter!   80
But come: I'll tell thee all my whole device
When I am in my coach, which stays for us
At the park gate; and therefore haste away,
For we must measure twenty miles today.   [*Exeunt*]

1   *look you:* you see

2-3   *the sins . . . children:* Children pay the penalties for their fathers'
          sins according to the Ten Commandments (*Exodus* 20:5).

3   *I fear you:* I fear for you, I am concerned about your welfare;
          plain: honest

4   *agitation:* Launcelot means *cogitation* (opinion).

7   *bastard hope:* false hope. Launcelot's pun expresses his true
          hope that Jessica may not be Shylock's legitimate daughter.

9-10   *got you not:* did not beget (father) you

11-12   *so the sins . . . upon me:* therefore, I would be punished for the
          sins of my mother (that is, adultery)

14-15   *Scylla . . . Charybdis:* These were famous monsters in classical
          mythology. Scylla snatched sailors from the decks of their ships
          as they tried to pass between her cave and the whirlpool of
          Charybdis. To be caught *between Scylla and Charybdis* is to
          find oneself trapped between two equally unpleasant and dan-
          gerous alternatives.

15   *gone:* doomed, lost

17   *I shall be . . . husband:* For the Biblical allusion, see *I Corinthians*
          7:14.

19-21   *We were Christians . . . one by another:* there were enough
          Christians before he converted you, just enough of us to live
          comfortably together

21-22   *This making of Christians . . . hogs:* Launcelot is wise enough
          to understand the economic laws of supply and demand. He
          is also aware that the dietary laws of the Old Testament for-
          bid the eating of pork. See Shylock's vow in Act 1, Scene 3,
          lines 30-31.

22-23   *we shall not . . . money:* soon we will not be able to buy bacon
          at any price

27   *corners:* secret or private places

28-29   *Launcelot and I are out:* we have had a quarrel

Scene 5

Belmont. Portia's garden

Enter Launcelot and Jessica

Launcelot: Yes, truly; for, look you, the sins of the father
are to be laid upon the children; therefore, I promise
you, I fear you. I was always plain with you, and so
now I speak my agitation of the matter: therefore be
o' good cheer; for, truly, I think you are damned.   5
There is but one hope in it that can do you any good,
and that is but a kind of bastard hope neither.
Jessica: And what hope is that, I pray thee?
Launcelot: Marry, you may partly hope that your father got
you not, that you are not the Jew's daughter.   10
Jessica: That were a kind of bastard hope, indeed: so the
sins of my mother should be visited upon me.
Launcelot: Truly then I fear you are damned both by father
and mother: thus when I shun Scylla (your father) I
fall into Charybdis (your mother): well, you are gone   15
both ways.
Jessica: I shall be saved by my husband; he hath made me
a Christian.
Launcelot: Truly the more to blame he: we were Christians
enow before; e'en as many as could well live one by   20
another. This making of Christians will raise the price
of hogs: if we grow all to be pork-eaters, we shall not
shortly have a rasher on the coals for money.
Enter Lorenzo
Jessica: I'll tell my husband, Launcelot, what you say: here
he comes.   25
Lorenzo: I shall grow jealous of you shortly, Launcelot, if
you thus get my wife into corners.
Jessica: Nay, you need not fear us, Lorenzo: Launcelot and
I are out. He tells me flatly there's no mercy for me in
heaven, because I am a Jew's daughter: and he says   30

31   *commonwealth:* state

34   *answer:* explain, justify

35   *getting up:* swelling

37   *Moor:* Moroccan woman (perhaps a servant in Portia's household)

37-38   *more than reason:* bigger than reasonable, bigger than she should be. Launcelot's pun depends upon the Elizabethan pronunciation of *Moor* as *more*.

38   *honest:* virtuous

41-42   *the best grace . . . parrots:* the best way to display one's intelligence will be to remain silent, and only parrots will be admired for their speaking

44   *they all have stomachs:* they are all hungry

45   *wit-snapper:* wisecracker

48   *cover:* set the table. The dinner has been prepared for some time already. In line 51, Launcelot jokingly misinterprets Lorenzo's repetition of the word as *put on your hat.* Launcelot would take his hat off as a sign of respect.

50   *quarrelling with occasion:* playing with words or quibbling at every opportunity

57   *humours and conceits:* whims and fancies

59   *discretion:* careful selection (of words)

62   *A many:* many; *stand in better place:* have better positions

63   *Garnish'd:* both "supplied" (with words) and "dressed" (in his serving liveries); *for:* for the sake of

64   *Defy the matter:* confuse the issue; *How cheer'st thou:* are you happy?

67   *Past all expressing:* More than I could say. *meet:* appropriate

68   *upright:* honourable

you are no good member of the commonwealth, for, in
converting Jews to Christians, you raise the price of
pork.

Lorenzo: I shall answer that better to the commonwealth
than you can the getting up of the negro's belly: the   35
Moor is with child by you, Launcelot.

Launcelot: It is much that the Moor should be more than
reason; but if she be less than an honest woman, she
is indeed more than I took her for.

Lorenzo: How every fool can play upon the word! I think   40
the best grace of wit will shortly turn into silence, and
discourse grow commendable in none only but parrots.
Go in, sirrah: bid them prepare for dinner.

Launcelot: That is done, sir; they have all stomachs.

Lorenzo: Goodly Lord, what a wit-snapper are you! then   45
bid them prepare dinner.

Launcelot: That is done too, sir; only 'cover' is the word.

Lorenzo: Will you cover, then, sir?

Launcelot: Not so, sir, neither; I know my duty.

Lorenzo: Yet more quarrelling with occasion! Wilt thou show   50
the whole wealth of thy wit in an instant? I pray thee,
understand a plain man in his plain meaning: go to
thy fellows; bid them cover the table, serve in the
meat, and we will come in to dinner.

Launcelot: For the table, sir, it shall be served in; for the   55
meat, sir, it shall be covered; for your coming in to
dinner, sir, why, let it be as humours and conceits
shall govern.   [*Exit*]

Lorenzo: O dear discretion, how his words are suited!
The fool hath planted in his memory   60
An army of good words, and I do know
A many fools, that stand in better place,
Garnish'd like him, that for a tricksy word
Defy the matter. How cheer'st thou, Jessica?
And now, good sweet, say thy opinion;   65
How dost thou like the Lord Bassanio's wife?

Jessica: Past all expressing. It is very meet
The Lord Bassanio live an upright life,
For, having such a blessing in his lady,
He finds the joys of heaven here on earth;   70

72   *In reason:* it makes sense that

74   *on the wager lay:* place as their bet

76   *pawn'd:* bet
77   *fellow:* equal

81   *anon:* soon

82   *stomach:* desire (both to eat and to praise you)

84   *howsome'er:* in whatever manner

86   *I'll set you forth:* I'll serve it to you. Jessica continues the
      metaphor of praise as food.

And if on earth he do not merit it,
In reason he should never come to heaven.
Why, if two gods should play some heavenly match,
And on the wager lay two earthly women,
And Portia one, there must be something else   75
Pawn'd with the other, for the poor rude world
Hath not her fellow.
Lorenzo: Even such a husband
Hast thou of me, as she is for a wife.
Jessica: Nay, but ask my opinion too of that.   80
Lorenzo: I will anon; first, let us go to dinner.
Jessica: Nay, let me praise you while I have a stomach.
Lorenzo: No, pray thee, let it serve for table-talk;
Then howsome'er thou speak'st, 'mong other things
I shall digest it.   85
Jessica: Well, I'll set you forth.
                                                  [*Exeunt*]

Act 3, Scenes 4 and 5: Activities

1. There are many possible variations in acting the role of Portia. In pairs, prepare two readings (one by each of you) of her speech on friendship (Scene 4, lines 10-23).

   Your two readings should present two *different* interpretations of Portia's character. She might sound sincere and generous, hypocritical and selfish, or even sarcastic.

   Whatever characteristics you choose to develop, your main tool should be your voice. Experiment with variations in pace, pitch, volume, and tone, as well as the use of pauses.

   Tape your readings or present them live to your class. Allow time for your classmates to compare their responses to your different versions of Portia. Discuss which versions are most convincing in light of the play's action so far.

2. Portia prepares us for an unexpected turn of events in her speeches to Balthazar and Nerissa in Scene 4. Put the clues together and predict the circumstances under which we will meet Portia and Nerissa again. Record your predictions in your journal, and check them for accuracy when you have completed your reading of the play.

3. Scene 5 provides our second view of Launcelot and Jessica in a "domestic" setting. List all the differences between this scene in Portia's house and the earlier scene outside Shylock's house (Act 2, Scene 5). Consider such features as the following:
   • humour
   • dramatic tone (mood of the scene)
   • character relationships
   • action
   • language use and word-play

Use your list to clarify how this scene supports Jessica's decision to leave her father's house and Launcelot's decision to leave Shylock's service.

For the next scene . . .

How do judges maintain order in court? Why do they some-times have difficulty with courtroom control? Why do lawyers raise objections to proceedings on behalf of their clients? How do lawyers sometimes go beyond the boundaries of proper courtroom behaviour?

Act 4, Scenes 1 and 2

In these scenes . . .

In the courtroom, Shylock demands that Antonio pay the penalty for failing to return the borrowed money on time. The Duke of Venice, who is acting as the judge in the case, encourages Shylock to show mercy to Antonio, but Shylock refuses. Bassanio offers to repay Shylock more than the sum Antonio borrowed, but Antonio has prepared himself to accept defeat – and death.

As Shylock is sharpening his knife to cut the pound of flesh from Antonio's breast, Portia arrives in court, disguised as Balthazar, a young but learned Doctor of Law. Portia renews the Duke's plea for mercy, but Shylock remains adamant. Without further delay, Portia decrees that Shylock is legally entitled to the pound of flesh. However, just as Shylock is about to take his revenge, Portia clarifies the exact wording of the bond, and Shylock's plan is defeated. Portia then points out that, under the law, Shylock should be punished for his attempt to injure Antonio. She insists that the court follow "the letter of the law" and show no mercy to Shylock, since he has been so insistent himself in carrying out the penalty agreed upon with Antonio. However, both the Duke and Antonio show mercy to Shylock as the trial comes to an end.

In gratitude for saving Antonio, Bassanio offers the young lawyer a gift. She demands his ring. At first Bassanio refuses, with much embarrassment, but Antonio encourages him to give the ring up. Nerissa, disguised as Balthazar's clerk, plans a way to trick Gratiano into giving his ring to her.

5   *void:* empty. Note the repetition for emphasis.

6   *dram:* small drop

7   *qualify:* modify, moderate; *obdurate:* stubborn, relentless

9-10   *And that no . . . envy's reach:* and I cannot be protected from his malice (*envy*) by the law

11   *arm'd:* prepared

13   *tyranny:* violence

16   *before our face:* in front of me. The plural pronoun was commonly used by royalty in Shakespeare's time.

18-19   *That thou . . . hour of act:* that you intend to make a show of relentless cruelty until the last possible moment

20   *remorse:* compassion, pity

21   *apparent:* seeming

22   *exact'st:* demand

24   *loose:* release, forget; *forfeiture:* penalty

26   *Forgive:* allow (Antonio) to keep; *moiety:* portion

Act 4, Scene 1

Venice. A court of justice

Enter the Duke, the Merchants,
Antonio, Bassanio, Gratiano,
Salerio, and Officers of the Court

Duke: What, is Antonio here?
Antonio: Ready, so please your Grace.
Duke: I am sorry for thee: thou art come to answer
  A stony adversary, an inhuman wretch
  Uncapable of pity, void and empty   5
  From any dram of mercy.
Antonio: I have heard
  Your Grace hath ta'en great pains to qualify
  His rigorous course; but since he stands obdurate,
  And that no lawful means can carry me
  Out of his envy's reach, I do oppose   10
  My patience to his fury, and am arm'd
  To suffer with a quietness of spirit
  The very tyranny and rage of his.
Duke: Go one, and call the Jew into the court.
Salerio: He is ready at the door: he comes, my lord.   15
  Enter Shylock
Duke: Make room, and let him stand before our face.
  Shylock, the world thinks, and I think so too,
  That thou but lead'st this fashion of thy malice
  To the last hour of act; and then 'tis thought
  Thou'lt show thy mercy and remorse more strange   20
  Than is thy strange apparent cruelty;
  And where thou now exact'st the penalty—
  Which is a pound of this poor merchant's flesh—
  Thou wilt not only loose the forfeiture,
  But, touch'd with human gentleness and love,   25
  Forgive a moiety of the principal,

29   *Enow:* enough

30   *commiseration of:* sympathy for

31   *brassy bosoms:* hearts as hard and as cold as brass

32   *Turks:* From medieval times until the early twentieth century, Turks were considered by Europeans to be savage and cruel. This stereotype was based upon the cruel practices of the Old Ottoman Empire.

      Tartars: The Asiatic tribes of this name are correctly called *Tatars.* Shakespeare's change probably reflects an association with Tartarus (Hades or Hell) in classical mythology. The Tatars, who travelled with Genghis Khan, were noted for their savagery.

32-33 *train'd To offices of:* taught to practise

35   *possess'd:* informed

36   *Sabbath:* the holiest day of the week, reserved for rest and prayer, as commanded by God in the Ten Commandments (*Exodus* 20: 8-11)

37   *due and forfeit:* proper penalty

38   *light:* descend, fall

39   *charter:* authority

41   *carrion:* rotten

43   *humour:* whim, fancy

46   *ban'd: baned* (poisoned), not *banned*

47   *gaping pig:* a roasted pig with an open mouth (often stuffed with an apple)

49   *sings i' the nose:* drones (with a nasal tone)

50   *affection:* personal taste, inclination

54-56 *he . . . he . . . he:* one man . . . another man . . . a third man

56   *woollen:* the leather bag of the Highland bagpipe is commonly wrapped in cotton or flannel

56-58 *but of force . . . being offended:* but he cannot prevent giving offence (that is, urinating in public) when he himself has been offended (by the bagpipe)

62   *A losing suit:* By pursuing the pound of flesh, Shylock will lose the money he lent to Antonio.

64   *current of thy cruelty:* the course that your cruelty is taking

Glancing an eye of pity on his losses,
That have of late so huddled on his back,
Enow to press a royal merchant down,
And pluck commiseration of his state   30
From brassy bosoms and rough hearts of flint,
From stubborn Turks and Tartars, never train'd
To offices of tender courtesy.
We all expect a gentle answer, Jew.
Shylock: I have possess'd your Grace of what I purpose;   35
And by our holy Sabbath have I sworn
To have the due and forfeit of my bond:
If you deny it, let the danger light
Upon your charter and your city's freedom.
You'll ask me, why I rather choose to have   40
A weight of carrion flesh than to receive
Three thousand ducats. I'll not answer that,
But say it is my humour. Is it answer'd?
What if my house be troubled with a rat,
And I be pleas'd to give ten thousand ducats   45
To have it ban'd? What, are you answer'd yet?
Some men there are love not a gaping pig;
Some, that are mad if they behold a cat;
And others, when the bagpipe sings i' the nose,
Cannot contain their urine: for affection,   50
Master of passion, sways it to the mood
Of what it likes, or loathes. Now, for your answer:
As there is no firm reason to be render'd,
Why he cannot abide a gaping pig;
Why he, a harmless necessary cat;   55
Why he, a woollen bagpipe, but of force
Must yield to such inevitable shame
As to offend, himself being offended;
So can I give no reason, nor I will not,
More than a lodg'd hate and a certain loathing   60
I bear Antonio, that I follow thus
A losing suit against him. Are you answer'd?
Bassanio: This is no answer, thou unfeeling man,
To excuse the current of thy cruelty.
Shylock: I am not bound to please thee with my answers.   65
Bassanio: Do all men kill the things they do not love?

68   *Every . . . first:* A single annoyance is not justifiable cause for hatred.

70   *think you question with:* remember that you are arguing with

72   *main flood:* high tide; *bate:* abate, reduce

73   *use question with:* ask

74   *ewe:* mother sheep; *bleat:* cry

76   *wag:* wave

77   *fretten:* fretted, blown

82   *conveniency:* efficiency

87   *draw:* accept

90   *You have . . . purchas'd slave:* Shylock's reference to slavery in Europe is intended to draw a comparison, not to question the practice of slavery itself. His point merely emphasizes the right of a property owner to use his property as he wishes.

92   *in abject . . . parts:* for base and servile jobs

97   *viands:* delicacies

100   *dearly:* at great expense

102   *force:* power, enforcement

104   *Upon:* in accordance with

105   *doctor:* lawyer. See the note for Act 3, Scene 4, line 50

106   *determine:* decide, settle

Shylock: Hates any man the thing he would not kill?
Bassanio: Every offence is not a hate at first.
Shylock: What! wouldst thou have a serpent sting thee twice?
Antonio: I pray you, think you question with the Jew: 70
    You may as well go stand upon the beach,
    And bid the main flood bate his usual height;
    You may as well use question with the wolf,
    Why he hath made the ewe bleat for the lamb;
    You may as well forbid the mountain pines   75
    To wag their high tops, and to make no noise
    When they are fretten with the gusts of heaven;
    You may as well do anything most hard,
    As seek to soften that—than which what's harder?—
    His Jewish heart: therefore, I do beseech you,   80
    Make no more offers, use no farther means;
    But with all brief and plain conveniency,
    Let me have judgment, and the Jew his will.
Bassanio: For thy three thousand ducats here is six.
Shylock: If every ducat in six thousand ducats   85
    Were in six parts, and every part a ducat,
    I would not draw them. I would have my bond.
Duke: How shalt thou hope for mercy, rendering none?
Shylock: What judgment shall I dread, doing no wrong?
    You have among you many a purchas'd slave,   90
    Which, like your asses and your dogs and mules,
    You use in abject and in slavish parts,
    Because you bought them: shall I say to you,
    'Let them be free, marry them to your heirs?
    Why sweat they under burdens? let their beds   95
    Be made as soft as yours, and let their palates
    Be season'd with such viands?' You will answer,
    'The slaves are ours'. So do I answer you:
    The pound of flesh which I demand of him,
    Is dearly bought; 'tis mine and I will have it.   100
    If you deny me, fie upon your law!
    There is no force in the decrees of Venice.
    I stand for judgment. Answer—shall I have it?
Duke: Upon my power I may dismiss this court,
    Unless Bellario, a learned doctor,   105
    Whom I have sent for to determine this,

109   *New:* recently, just this minute

114   *tainted:* diseased; *wether:* ram

115   *Meetest:* most suitable

118   *live still:* continue living; *epitaph:* inscription on a tombstone, often in praise of the dead person

121   *whet:* sharpen. The lines which follow indicate that Shylock is using the leather sole of his shoe to sharpen his knife.

124   *keen:* sharp

125   *hangman:* executioner. Beheading, rather than hanging, was the most common form of capital punishment in Shakespeare's day. *Hangman* was a term used for an executioner of any type.

126   *envy:* malice, hatred

128   *inexecrable:* unable to be cursed. Gratiano suggests that Shylock is so evil that no curse adequately condemns him.

129   *for thy life . . . accused:* it is unjust that you are allowed to live (justice deserves to be found guilty for allowing you to live)

130   *my faith:* Gratiano's faith is Christianity, which does not allow a belief in reincarnation.

131   *hold opinion:* agree; *Pythagoras:* Pythagoras was a Greek philosopher and mathematician of the sixth century B.C. who believed that the souls of the dead were reborn in the bodies of other humans or animals. His skills as a mathematician led to the discovery of the geometric law known today as the Pythagorean theorem.

132   *infuse:* pour

133   *trunks:* bodies; *currish:* like a cur (mongrel dog)

134   *hang'd for human slaughter:* In Shakespeare's time, animals suspected of killing or attacking humans were actually hanged.

135   *Even:* directly; *fell:* cruel; *fleet:* fly away

136   *unhallow'd:* unholy (un-Christian); *dam:* mother

139   *rail:* shout

140   *offend'st:* injure

143   *commend:* recommend

Come here today.

Salerio: My lord, here stays without
A messenger with letters from the doctor,
New come from Padua.

Duke: Bring us the letters: call the messenger.   110

Bassanio: Good cheer, Antonio! What, man, courage yet!
The Jew shall have my flesh, blood, bones, and all,
Ere thou shalt lose for me one drop of blood.

Antonio: I am a tainted wether of the flock,
Meetest for death: the weakest kind of fruit   115
Drops earliest to the ground; and so let me.
You cannot better be employ'd, Bassanio,
Than to live still, and write mine epitaph.

Enter Nerissa, dressed like a lawyer's clerk

Duke: Came you from Padua, from Bellario?

Nerissa: From both, my lord. Bellario greets your Grace.   120
                               [Presents a letter]

Bassanio: Why dost thou whet thy knife so earnestly?

Shylock: To cut the forfeiture from that bankrupt there.

Gratiano: Not on thy sole, but on thy soul, harsh Jew,
Thou mak'st thy knife keen; but no metal can,
No, not the hangman's axe, bear half the keenness   125
Of thy sharp envy. Can no prayers pierce thee?

Shylock: No, none that thou hast wit enough to make.

Gratiano: O, be thou damn'd, inexecrable dog!
And for thy life let justice be accus'd.
Thou almost mak'st me waver in my faith   130
To hold opinion with Pythagoras,
That souls of animals infuse themselves
Into the trunks of men: thy currish spirit
Govern'd a wolf, who, hang'd for human slaughter,
Even from the gallows did his fell soul fleet,   135
And whilst thou lay'st in thy unhallow'd dam,
Infus'd itself in thee; for thy desires
Are wolvish, bloody, starv'd, and ravenous.

Shylock: Till thou canst rail the seal from off my bond.
Thou but offend'st thy lungs to speak so loud: 140
Repair thy wit, good youth, or it will fall
To cureless ruin. I stand here for law.

Duke: This letter from Bellario doth commend

145   *hard by:* nearby

148   *conduct:* escort

154   *cause:* case, matter

156   *turn'd over:* looked through; *is furnish'd with:* has been given

157   *bettered:* improved

159   *importunity:* request

160   *in my stead:* in my place

160-162 *let his lack . . . reverend estimation:* do not let his youth be an obstacle to your high opinion of him

164   *trial . . . commendation:* when you use him, you will discover how much his worth exceeds my praise

169   *difference:* dispute

171   *throughly:* thoroughly

176   *in such rule:* so within the law

177   *impugn:* find fault with, oppose

A young and learned doctor to our court.
Where is he?   145
Nerissa: He attendeth here hard by,
To know your answer, whether you'll admit him.
Duke: With all my heart: some three or four of you
Go give him courteous conduct to this place.
                                        [*Exeunt Officers*]
Meantime, the court shall hear Bellario's letter.

Your Grace shall understand that at the receipt of your letter 150
I am very sick; but in the instant that your messenger came,
in loving visitation was with me a young doctor of Rome;
his name is Balthazar. I acquainted him with the cause
in controversy between the Jew and Antonio the
merchant. We turned o'er many books together. He is   155
furnished with my opinion; which, bettered with his own
learning—the greatness whereof I cannot enough
commend—comes with him, at my importunity, to fill up
your Grace's request in my stead. I beseech you, let his
lack of years be no impediment to let him lack a reverend   160
estimation, for I never knew so young a body with so old
a head. I leave him to your gracious acceptance, whose trial
shall better publish his commendation.

Enter Portia, dressed like a doctor of law
You hear the learn'd Bellario, what he writes:
And here, I take it, is the doctor come.   165
Give me your hand. Come you from old Bellario?
Portia: I did, my lord.
Duke: You are welcome: take your place.
Are you acquainted with the difference
That holds this present question in the court?   170
Portia: I am informed throughly of the cause.
Which is the merchant here, and which the Jew?
Duke: Antonio and old Shylock, both stand forth.
Portia: Is your name Shylock?
Shylock: Shylock is my name.
Portia: Of a strange nature is the suit you follow;   175
Yet in such rule, that the Venetian law
Cannot impugn you as you do proceed.

178   *within his danger:* in his power

180   *Then must . . . merciful:* Portia suggests to Antonio that Shylock's mercy is his only hope. Shylock's interruption indicates that he interprets her *must* as a command.

181   *On what . . . that:* What will force me to be merciful?

182   *quality:* trait, virtue, human characteristic; *is not strain'd:* cannot be forced

184   *it is twice blessed:* it blesses twice

186   *becomes:* suits

188   *shows:* represents, symbolizes; *temporal:* earthly, in time (that is, not eternal)

189   *attribute to:* symbol of

190   *Wherein . . . kings:* When we see the king's sceptre, we are reminded of his authority over us and, therefore, respect and fear his power

191   *above this sceptred sway:* is greater than the temporal power represented by the sceptre

195   *seasons:* moderates

196   *Though . . . plea:* although you are asking for justice

197-198   *That in the course . . . mercy:* If God pursued justice without mercy (as you do), no man or woman would be saved (from eternal damnation).

201   *mitigate:* soften, moderate

204   *My deeds upon my head:* I take full responsibility for what I am doing. *crave:* demand

206   *discharge:* repay

207   *tender:* offer

209   *I will be bound:* I will sign a legal agreement

212   *bears down:* crushes, destroys

213   *Wrest:* twist, bend; *once:* on this one occasion; *to:* with

215   *curb:* restrain

[*To Antonio*] You stand within his danger, do you not?
Antonio: Ay, so he says.
Portia: Do you confess the bond?
Antonio: I do. 180
Portia: Then must the Jew be merciful.
Shylock: On what compulsion must I? tell me that.
Portia: The quality of mercy is not strain'd;
   It droppeth as the gentle rain from heaven
   Upon the place beneath: it is twice bless'd;
   It blesseth him that gives and him that takes. 185
   'Tis mightiest in the mightiest: it becomes
   The throned monarch better than his crown;
   His sceptre shows the force of temporal power,
   The attribute to awe and majesty,
   Wherein doth sit the dread and fear of kings: 190
   But mercy is above this sceptred sway,
   It is enthroned in the hearts of kings,
   It is an attribute to God himself,
   And earthly power doth then show likest God's
   When mercy seasons justice. Therefore, Jew, 195
   Though justice be thy plea, consider this,
   That in the course of justice none of us
   Should see salvation: we do pray for mercy,
   And that same prayer doth teach us all to render
   The deeds of mercy. I have spoke thus much 200
   To mitigate the justice of thy plea,
   Which if thou follow, this strict court of Venice
   Must needs give sentence 'gainst the merchant there.
Shylock: My deeds upon my head! I crave the law,
   The penalty and forfeit of my bond. 205
Portia: Is he not able to discharge the money?
Bassanio: Yes, here I tender it for him in the court;
   Yea, twice the sum: if that will not suffice,
   I will be bound to pay it ten times o'er,
   On forfeit of my hands, my head, my heart. 210
   If this will not suffice, it must appear
   That malice bears down truth. And, I beseech you,
   Wrest once the law to your authority:
   To do a great right, do a little wrong,
   And curb this cruel devil of his will. 215

221 *Daniel:* A Daniel is one who displays wisdom beyond his years. The History of Susannah tells how Susannah rejected the advances of two elders, was falsely accused by them, and condemned to death. They claimed to have seen her lying under a tree with a young man. Daniel established Susannah's innocence – and the hypocrisy of the elders – by asking both accusers under what kind of tree the adultery had taken place. Each named a different tree.

226 *An oath:* Shylock means the oath referred to in line 36.

233 *tenor:* wording or details (of a legal document)

235 *exposition:* interpretation, explanation

246 *Hath full relation to:* supports fully

249 *elder:* more mature (hence, wiser)

Portia: It must not be. There is no power in Venice
　Can alter a decree established:
　'Twill be recorded for a precedent,
　And many an error by the same example
　Will rush into the state. It cannot be.　　　　　　220
Shylock: A Daniel come to judgment! yea, a Daniel!
　O wise young judge, how I do honour thee!
Portia: I pray you, let me look upon the bond.
Shylock: Here 'tis, most reverend doctor, here it is.
Portia: Shylock, there's thrice thy money offer'd thee.　225
Shylock: An oath, an oath, I have an oath in heaven;
　Shall I lay perjury upon my soul?
　No, not for Venice.
Portia:　　　　　　　　　　Why, this bond is forfeit;
　And lawfully by this the Jew may claim
　A pound of flesh, to be by him cut off　　　　　230
　Nearest the merchant's heart. Be merciful:
　Take thrice thy money; bid me tear the bond.
Shylock: When it is paid according to the tenour.
　It doth appear you are a worthy judge;
　You know the law, your exposition　　　　　235
　Hath been most sound: I charge you by the law,
　Whereof you are a well-deserving pillar,
　Proceed to judgment: by my soul I swear
　There is no power in the tongue of man
　To alter me. I stay here on my bond.　　　　　240
　Most heartily I do beseech the court
　To give the judgment
Portia:　　　　　　　　　Why then, thus it is:
　You must prepare your bosom for his knife.
Shylock: O noble judge! O excellent young man!
Portia: For, the intent and purpose of the law　　245
　Hath full relation to the penalty,
　Which here appeareth due upon the bond.
Shylock: 'Tis very true! O wise and upright judge!
　How much more elder art thou than thy looks!
Portia: Therefore lay bare your bosom.　　　　　250
Shylock:　　　　　　　　　　Ay, 'his breast':
　So says the bond:—doth it not, noble judge?—
　'Nearest his heart'—those are the very words.

253   *balance:* scales

255   *on your charge:* at your expense

257   *nominated:* specified

259   *for charity:* out of goodness

265   *Fortune:* Fors Fortuna was the classical goddess of chance or luck. In medieval times, she was usually pictured with her wheel of fortune.

266   *still her use:* her usual habit

269   *An age of poverty:* a poverty-stricken old age; *penance:* punishment

273   *speak me fair in death:* speak kindly of me when I am dead

276   *Repent:* regret

281   *Which:* who

285   *deliver:* save

287   *by:* nearby

289   *I would she were in heaven:* To be in heaven, of course, Nerissa would have to be dead!

Portia: It is so. Are there balance here to weigh
  The flesh?
Shylock: I have them ready.
Portia: Have by some surgeon, Shylock, on your charge,   255
  To stop his wounds, lest he do bleed to death.
Shylock: Is it so nominated in the bond?
Portia: It is not so express'd; but what of that?
  'Twere good you do so much for charity.
Shylock: I cannot find it: 'tis not in the bond.   260
Portia: You, merchant, have you anything to say?
Antonio: But little: I am arm'd and well prepar'd.
  Give me your hand, Bassanio: fare you well!
  Grieve not that I am fall'n to this for you,
  For herein Fortune shows herself more kind   265
  Than is her custom: it is still her use
  To let the wretched man outlive his wealth,
  To view with hollow eye and wrinkled brow
  An age of poverty; from which lingering penance
  Of such misery doth she cut me off.   270
  Commend me to your honourable wife.
  Tell her the process of Antonio's end;
  Say how I lov'd you, speak me fair in death;
  And, when the tale is told, bid her be judge
  Whether Bassanio had not once a love.   275
  Repent but you that you shall lose your friend,
  And he repents not that he pays your debt;
  For if the Jew do cut but deep enough,
  I'll pay it instantly with all my heart.
Bassanio: Antonio, I am married to a wife   280
  Which is as dear to me as life itself;
  But life itself, my wife, and all the world,
  Are not with me esteem'd above thy life:
  I would lose all, ay, sacrifice them all,
  Here to this devil, to deliver you.   285
Portia: Your wife would give you little thanks for that,
  If she were by to hear you make the offer.
Gratiano: I have a wife, who, I protest, I love:
  I would she were in heaven, so she could
  Entreat some power to change this currish Jew.   290
Nerissa: 'Tis well you offer it behind her back;

294   *stock:* breed; *Barrabas:* Barabbas was the thief who was released when Jesus was crucified (*Matthew* 27: 15-23). Shakespeare's spelling points to the appropriate metrical pronunciation (with the accent on the first syllable).

280-295 *Antonio . . . Christian:* What might be Shakespeare's purposes for this digression?

296   *trifle:* waste; *pursue sentence:* proceed to a decision

303   *Tarry:* wait

304   *jot:* drop

309   *confiscate:* confiscated, taken as a legal penalty

312   *act:* written decree

313   *urgest:* demand

318   *Soft:* roughly, "Slow down!" or "Keep quiet!"

319   *all:* nothing but

321   *upright:* honest

324   *just:* exactly

325   *just:* exact

326   *substance:* weight

328   *scruple:* a very small unit of weight

329   *estimation:* amount (here, breadth)

The wish would make else an unquiet house.
Shylock: These be the Christian husbands! I have a daughter;
Would any of the stock of Barrabas
Had been her husband rather than a Christian!   295
We trifle time; I pray thee, pursue sentence.
Portia: A pound of that same merchant's flesh is thine:
The court awards it, and the law doth give it.
Shylock: Most rightful judge!
Portia: And you must cut this flesh from off his breast: 300
The law allows it, and the court awards it.
Shylock: Most learned judge! A sentence! come, prepare!
Portia: Tarry a little: there is something else.
This bond doth give thee here no jot of blood;
The words expressly are 'a pound of flesh':   305
Take then thy bond, take thou thy pound of flesh;
But, in the cutting it, if thou dost shed
One drop of Christian blood, thy lands and goods
Are, by the laws of Venice, confiscate
Unto the state of Venice.   310
Gratiano: O upright judge! Mark, Jew: O learned judge!
Shylock: Is that the law?
Portia: Thyself shall see the act;
For, as thou urgest justice, be assur'd
Thou shalt have justice more than thou desir'st.
Gratiano: O learned judge! Mark, Jew: a learned judge!   315
Shylock: I take this offer then: pay the bond thrice,
And let the Christian go.
Bassanio: Here is the money.
Portia: Soft!
The Jew shall have all justice; soft! no haste:—
He shall have nothing but the penalty.   320
Gratiano: O Jew! an upright judge, a learned judge!
Portia: Therefore prepare thee to cut off the flesh.
Shed thou no blood; nor cut thou less, nor more,
But just a pound of flesh: if thou tak'st more,
Or less, than a just pound, be it but so much   325
As makes it light or heavy in the substance,
Or the division of the twentieth part
Of one poor scruple, nay, if the scale do turn
But in the estimation of a hair,

332   *on the hip:* at a disadvantage, at my mercy. Compare Shylock's earlier threat (Act 1, Scene 3, line 42)

334   *principal:* original sum borrowed (3000 ducats)

343   *give him good of it:* help him to enjoy it

344   *question:* to argue

346   *enacted:* decreed

347   *alien:* non-citizen. Even if he were born in Venice, Shylock would not be a Venetian citizen, for Jews were not granted citizenship in most states of medieval Europe.

350   *party:* person. Portia's use of legal jargon suggests that she may have memorized the appropriate law. *contrive:* plot

352   *privy coffer:* state treasury (originally, for the private use of the sovereign)

354   *'gainst all other voice:* regardless of any other opinion

356   *by manifest proceeding:* from the obvious events of the enquiry

359   *incurr'd:* run into

360   *rehears'd:* outlined, reviewed

366   *That:* so that, in order that

Thou diest, and all thy goods are confiscate.   330
Gratiano: A second Daniel, a Daniel, Jew!
  Now, infidel, I have you on the hip.
Portia: Why doth the Jew pause? take thy forfeiture.
Shylock: Give me my principal, and let me go.
Bassanio: I have it ready for thee; here it is.   335
Portia: He hath refus'd it in the open court:
  He shall have merely justice, and his bond.
Gratiano: A Daniel, still say I; a second Daniel!
  I thank thee, Jew, for teaching me that word.
Shylock: Shall I not have barely my principal?   340
Portia: Thou shalt have nothing but the forfeiture,
  To be so taken at thy peril, Jew.
Shylock: Why, then the devil give him good of it!
  I'll stay no longer question.
Portia: Tarry, Jew:
  The law hath yet another hold on you.   345
  It is enacted in the laws of Venice,
  If it be prov'd against an alien
  That by direct or indirect attempts
  He seek the life of any citizen,
  The party 'gainst the which he doth contrive   350
  Shall seize one half his goods; the other half
  Comes to the privy coffer of the state;
  And the offender's life lies in the mercy
  Of the duke only, 'gainst all other voice.
  In which predicament, I say, thou stand'st;   355
  For it appears by manifest proceeding,
  That indirectly, and directly too,
  Thou hast contriv'd against the very life
  Of the defendant; and thou hast incurr'd
  The danger formerly by me rehears'd.   360
  Down therefore and beg mercy of the duke.
Gratiano: Beg that thou may'st have leave to hang thyself—
  And yet, thy wealth being forfeit to the state,
  Thou hast not left the value of a cord;
  Therefore thou must be hang'd at the state's charge.   365
Duke: That thou shalt see the difference of our spirit,
  I pardon thee thy life before thou ask it.
  For half thy wealth, it is Antonio's;

369   *general state:* general use of the state

370   *humbleness:* on Shylock's part; *drive into:* reduce to

373   *prop:* supporting pillar or beam

377   *halter:* hangman's noose; *gratis:* free of interest

378   *So please:* if it pleases

379   *quit:* cancel

380   *So:* as long as, provided that

381   *in use:* in trust (to use as I see fit)

385   *presently:* immediately. Though Antonio's demand seems unmerciful and even unreasonable to a modern audience, earlier Christian audiences would have seen it as an act of charity. They would have believed that Shylock's conversion would save his soul from eternal damnation. This issue was treated comically in the earlier scene between Launcelot and Jessica (Act 3, Scene 5, lines 1-19).

387   *all he dies possess'd:* all he owns when he dies

389   *recant:* withdraw, retract

390   *late:* recently

392   *I am content:* Does Shylock have any alternative?

396   *god-fathers:* Christian parents select a pair of close friends or relatives to help them in the spiritual education of their children. These *godparents* begin to play their role at the ceremony of baptism. In the next line, Gratiano jokingly refers to the twelve *god-fathers* who make up the twelve-man jury in a court of law. Gratiano claims that, had he been the judge, his jury would have condemned Shylock to death.

398   *font:* the basin, usually of stone, which holds the holy water used in the ceremony of baptism (referring here to Shylock's conversion)

402   *meet:* necessary

403   *your leisure serves you not:* you cannot afford time for relaxation

404   *gratify:* show your gratitude toward, reward

405   *bound:* indebted

The other half comes to the general state,
Which humbleness may drive unto a fine.   370
Portia: Ay, for the state; not for Antonio.
Shylock: Nay, take my life and all; pardon not that:
You take my house, when you do take the prop
That doth sustain my house; you take my life
When you do take the means whereby I live.   375
Portia: What mercy can you render him, Antonio?
Gratiano: A halter gratis; nothing else, for God's sake!
Antonio: So please my lord the duke, and all the court,
To quit the fine for one half of his goods,
I am content so he will let me have   380
The other half in use, to render it,
Upon his death, unto the gentleman
That lately stole his daughter.
Two things provided more, that, for this favour,
He presently become a Christian;   385
The other, that he do record a gift,
Here in the court, of all he dies possess'd,
Unto his son Lorenzo and his daughter.
Duke: He shall do this, or else I do recant
The pardon that I late pronounced here.   390
Portia: Art thou contented, Jew? what dost thou say?
Shylock: I am content.
Portia: Clerk, draw a deed of gift.
Shylock: I pray you give me leave to go from hence:
I am not well. Send the deed after me,
And I will sign it.   395
Duke: Get thee gone, but do it.
Gratiano: In christening shalt thou have two god-fathers;
Had I been judge, thou shouldst have had ten more,
To bring thee to the gallows, not to the font.
                              [*Exit Shylock*]
Duke: Sir, I entreat you home with me to dinner.
Portia: I humbly do desire your Grace of pardon: 400
I must away this night toward Padua,
And it is meet I presently set forth.
Duke: I am sorry that your leisure serves you not.
Antonio, gratify this gentleman,
For, in my mind, you are much bound to him.   405

408   *in lieu whereof:* in return for which

410   *freely:* willingly; *cope:* match (give as an equivalent for)

416   *mercenary:* interested in money

417   *know:* recognize

419   *of force:* it is necessary; *attempt you further:* try harder to persuade you

420   *tribute:* token of respect

422   *Not to . . . pardon me:* Not to refuse my request and to excuse my insistence

423   *You press me far:* you are very insistent

424   *Give me . . . sake:* This line is probably spoken to Antonio, the next obviously to Bassanio.

431   *And now . . . to it:* and now I have made up my mind to have it

432   *There's more . . . the value:* More than the cost of the ring itself is at stake

433   *dearest:* most expensive

434   *by proclamation:* with a public announcement (that I will buy it)

435   *for this:* for this particular ring

436   *liberal in offers:* generous in making promises (not in keeping them)

442   *'scuse:* excuse

[*Exeunt Duke, Merchants, and Officers of the Court*]
Bassanio: Most worthy gentleman, I and my friend
   Have by your wisdom been this day acquitted
   Of grievous penalties, in lieu whereof,
   Three thousand ducats, due unto the Jew,
   We freely cope your courteous pains withal.   410
Antonio: And stand indebted, over and above,
   In love and service to you evermore.
Portia: He is well paid that is well satisfied,
   And I, delivering you, am satisfied,
   And therein do account myself well paid: 415
   My mind was never yet more mercenary.
   I pray you, know me when we meet again:
   I wish you well, and so I take my leave.
Bassanio: Dear sir, of force I must attempt you further:
   Take some remembrance of us as a tribute,   420
   Not as a fee. Grant me two things, I pray you,
   Not to deny me, and to pardon me.
Portia: You press me far, and therefore I will yield.
   Give me your gloves, I'll wear them for your sake;
   And (for your love) I'll take this ring from you.   425
   Do not draw back your hand; I'll take no more,
   And you in love shall not deny me this.
Bassanio: This ring, good sir? alas! it is a trifle.
   I will not shame myself to give you this.
Portia: I will have nothing else but only this;   430
   And now methinks I have a mind to it.
Bassanio: There's more depends on this than on the value.
   The dearest ring in Venice will I give you,
   And find it out by proclamation:
   Only for this, I pray you, pardon me.   435
Portia. I see, sir, you are liberal in offers:
   You taught me first to beg, and now methinks
   You teach me how a beggar should be answer'd.
Bassanio: Good sir, this ring was given me by my wife,
   And, when she put it on, she made me vow   440
   That I should neither sell, nor give nor lose it.
Portia: That 'scuse serves many men to save their gifts.
   And if your wife be not a mad-woman,
   And know how well I have deserv'd this ring,

445   *hold out enemy:* be angry with you

449   *'gainst:* more highly than

453   *You and I will thither:* we will go there

She would not hold out enemy for ever,   445
For giving it to me. Well, peace be with you.

[Exeunt Portia and Nerissa]

Antonio: My Lord Bassanio, let him have the ring:
Let his deservings and my love withal
Be valu'd 'gainst your wife's commandement.

Bassanio: Go, Gratiano; run and overtake him;   450
Give him the ring, and bring him, if thou canst,
Unto Antonio's house. Away, make haste.

[Exit Gratiano]

Come, you and I will thither presently,
And in the morning early will we both
Fly toward Belmont. Come, Antonio.   *[Exeunt]* 455

1   *this deed:* the deed of gift arranged in the previous scene
     (line 392)

5   *o'erta'en:* overtaken

6   *upon more advice:* after further consideration

15   *I warrant:* I guarantee; *old:* abundant

17   *outface:* outdo them in insisting. What then does *outswear* mean?

Scene 2

Venice. A street

Enter Portia and Nerissa

Portia: Inquire the Jew's house out, give him this deed,
And let him sign it. We'll away tonight,
And be a day before our husbands home:
This deed will be well welcome to Lorenzo.
Enter Gratiano
Gratiano: Fair sir, you are well o'erta'en.   5
My Lord Bassanio, upon more advice,
Hath sent you here this ring, and doth entreat
Your company at dinner.
Portia: That cannot be.
His ring I do accept most thankfully,
And so, I pray you, tell him: furthermore,   10
I pray you, show my youth old Shylock's house.
Gratiano: That will I do.
Nerissa: Sir, I would speak with you.
[*Aside to Portia*] I'll see if I can get my husband's ring,
Which I did make him swear to keep for ever.
Portia: Thou may'st, I warrant. We shall have old swearing   15
That they did give the rings away to men;
But we'll outface them, and outswear them too.
Away, make haste! thou know'st where I will tarry.
Nerissa: Come, good sir, will you show me to this house?
                                        [*Exeunt*]

Act 4, Scenes 1 and 2: Activities

1. So can I give no reason, nor I will not,
   More than a lodg'd hate and a certain loathing
   I bear Antonio . . . (Scene 1, lines 59-61)

   Earlier in the play, Shylock has outlined his complaints against Antonio: once to himself (Act 1, Scene 3, lines 37-48) and once under great emotional stress (Act 3, Scene 1, lines 49-69). Why do you think he does not explain his reasons when asked in open court? Record your first thoughts in your journal. Then, compare notes and discuss your opinions with a partner.

2. Reread Antonio's speech beginning, "I pray you, think you question with the Jew . . . " (Scene 1, lines 70-83). How do the images Antonio uses confirm our impression of his prejudice? What effect would this speech have upon Shylock?

3. Early in Scene 1, Shylock claims that Antonio's pound of flesh has been "dearly bought" (line 100). In a small group, make a list of all the "payments" you think Shylock has made for the pound of flesh.

4. You cannot better be employed, Bassanio,
   Than to live still, and write mine epitaph.
   (Scene 1, lines 117-118)

   In Shakespeare's time and earlier, epitaphs often took the form of short poems, written by friends or relatives of the dead person. For example:

   > Here lies John Goddard, maker of bellows,
   > His craft's master, and king of good fellows;
   > But for all that, he came to his death,
   > For he that made bellows could not make breath.

   Sometimes they relate to an outstanding character trait:

   > Within this place lies Abraham the civil,
   > Who never did good, who never did evil –
   > Too ill then for God, too good for the Devil.

Some epitaphs seem to have been written merely to appeal to the reader's sense of humour:

An Epitaph on a Man for Doing Nothing

Here lies the man was born, and cried,
Told threescore years, fell sick, and died.

As Bassanio, write the epitaph which would be appropriate to Antonio at this moment in the play. Try also to compose epitaphs by Gratiano and the Duke (or even Shylock!) at this same point in the play.

5. Portia's speech on the "quality of mercy" (lines 180-201) is based upon the Christian belief that, since no one is free of sin, everyone requires God's mercy to be saved from eternal damnation. In other words, no one is perfect, but we can aspire to godliness through "God-like" acts of mercy. Shylock misunderstands: he has done nothing *illegal*, and so, he feels, he has no need of mercy.

If you could stop the hearing and talk to Shylock, what would you say to help him understand Portia's speech more fully?

a) Record your first thoughts in your journal.

b) In small groups, discuss the meaning of Portia's speech in order to clarify and organize your thoughts.

c) Deliver your speech for Shylock to the group or to the class.

6. "To do a great right, do a little wrong . . ." (line 214) As a class activity, discuss Bassanio's request. In your discussion, consider the following questions: In what situations, if any, might you advise "doing a little wrong" in order to achieve a greater good? Would you lie to protect a friend? Would you steal to feed a starving child? Why does Portia reject Bassanio's argument? Do you agree with her reasoning or with Bassanio's?

7. Debate in parliamentary style: Be it resolved that, in the courtroom scene, Bassanio finally shows qualities and values which make him deserving of Portia's love.

8. Portia's judgment that "this bond doth give thee no jot of blood" (line 304) marks a turning point in the courtroom scene. Shylock is given very little opportunity to express in words his reaction to this turn of events. Clearly, the actor who plays Shylock has to convey his changing responses through actions.

   In a director's log, make notes to describe what emotions you expect the actor to show from the turning point of this scene to its conclusion. Use the few lines of speech that Shylock does have as a guide. Note also the final impression of Shylock which the actor should convey to the audience. How should the audience feel about Shylock's defeat?

9. "Love thy neighbour as thyself" (*Matthew* 22:39)

   Toward the end of the hearing, Antonio and the Duke both display the spirit of "Christian love" or charity prescribed in Jesus' commandment.

   a) In your notebook, outline the acts of mercy which Antonio and the Duke show to Shylock (lines 366-390). Be sure to consider the exact terms of Shylock's sentence.

   b) In a small group, assess the fairness of Shylock's sentence in a *modern* context.

10. You are a lawyer representing either Shylock or Antonio at this courtroom hearing. From what you know of legal procedure, either from experience or from television and film, identify those statements and actions through-out the hearing to which you would object on behalf of your client. In each case, state the grounds of your objection.

In groups of three, play out short sections of the hearing. Two lawyers should insert objections on behalf of their clients, Antonio and Shylock, and the judge should sustain or overrule the objections.

11. a) In pairs, prepare and make an audio or video recording of a news interview with Portia/Balthazar after the court hearing. Plan your questions carefully in advance, designing them to cover the range of your viewers' or listeners' interests. Be sure to find out why she put Antonio through so much anxiety before revealing the legal argument that she knew would foil Shylock's plan.

    b) Conduct a similar interview with Antonio. Your viewers or listeners will have a wide range of questions for him as well. In particular, they will want to know about his thoughts at the point of death, his relief at his escape, and his decision to be merciful to the enemy who had just tried to kill him.

    c) On your own, use these interviews to prepare a feature article on the hearing for a newspaper or newsmagazine.

12. What reasons might Shakespeare have had for including the device of the "ring plot" immediately following the courtroom scene? As Shakespeare, record your reasons in a journal entry.

For the next scene . . .

"Music hath charms . . ." How important is music to you? What effects does it have upon you? How does it add to your life?

Act 5, Scene 1

In this scene . . .

Lorenzo and Jessica wander in the moonlit gardens of Belmont. They compare themselves to other pairs of famous lovers and comment on the soothing power of beautiful music. Portia and Nerissa arrive home from Venice, just before their husbands return to Belmont.

Before long, Portia and Nerissa steer the conversation to the topic of the wedding rings, and a heated argument begins when Bassanio and Gratiano admit that they have given the rings away. After much teasing, Portia reveals the true identities of Balthazar and his clerk. She adds to the merriment by announcing that three of Antonio's ships have returned safely and by presenting Jessica and Lorenzo with the contract by which they will inherit Shylock's wealth. In a mood of celebration, the company leaves the stage.

4   *Troilus:* During the Trojan War, young Troilus was separated from Cressida when she was taken hostage and carried off to the Greek encampment. The pair had vowed to be faithful to one another, and Troilus has become a symbol of the faithful lover.

7   *Thisbe:* The love between Pyramus and Thisbe was forbidden by their parents. They planned to meet by moonlight in the woods. Arriving first, Thisbe was frightened by a lion and sought safety in a nearby cave. The lion mauled the scarf which she had dropped in her panic. Finding the scarf, Pyramus assumed Thisbe had been killed and stabbed himself. In her grief, Thisbe took her own life. *o'ertrip:* step lightly over, dance over

8   *ere himself:* before she saw the lion

10   *Dido:* The queen of Carthage who was deserted by her lover Aeneas when his sense of duty compelled him to set sail for Italy; *willow:* The willow tree is symbolic of grief.

11   *waft:* waved to

13   *Medea:* The young princess who fled from Colchis with Jason and the golden fleece. Later, she used her magical powers to rejuvenate Jason's father, Aeson.

15   *steal:* What is the pun?

16   *unthrift love:* penniless lover (Lorenzo). Lorenzo might also be joking about Jessica's unwise affection for him.

19   *stealing:* taking possession of

21   *shrew:* a scolding, bad-tempered woman

23   *out-night:* Jessica invents the verb for this occasion. What does she mean? Compare *outface* and *outswear* in the previous scene (line 17).

Act 5, Scene 1

*Belmont. The garden in front of
Portia's house*

Enter Lorenzo and Jessica

Lorenzo: The moon shines bright: in such a night as this,
When the sweet wind did gently kiss the trees,
And they did make no noise, in such a night
Troilus methinks mounted the Trojan walls,
And sigh'd his soul toward the Grecian tents,   5
Where Cressid lay that night.
Jessica: In such a night
Did Thisbe fearfully o'ertrip the dew,
And saw the lion's shadow ere himself,
And ran dismay'd away.
Lorenzo: In such a night
Stood Dido with a willow in her hand   10
Upon the wild sea-banks, and waft her love
To come again to Cathage.
Jessica: In such a night
Medea gather'd the enchanted herbs
That did renew old Æson.
Lorenzo: In such a night
Did Jessica steal from the wealthy Jew,   15
And with an unthrift love did run from Venice,
As far as Belmont.
Jessica: In such a night
Did young Lorenzo swear he lov'd her well,
Stealing her soul with many vows of faith,
And ne'er a true one.   20
Lorenzo: In such a night
Did pretty Jessica, like a little shrew,
Slander her love, and he forgave it her.
Jessica: I would out-night you, did nobody come;

24   *footing:* footsteps

31   *holy crosses:* small roadside shrines where travellers could pray

39   *Sola, sola!:* Launcelot imitates the sound of a posthorn or bugle. *Sola* seems to be a combination of *soh* and *lah*, two of the eight notes on the musical scale. The *wo ha, ho!* addresses his make-believe horse and commands it to stop.

43   *Leave hollowing:* stop shouting

46   *post:* messenger

49   *expect:* await

51   *signify:* announce

57   *Become:* suit

59   *patens:* small discs of shiny metal (that is, the stars)

But, hark! I hear the footing of a man.
Enter Stephano
Lorenzo: Who comes so fast in silence of the night?   25
Stephano: A friend.
Lorenzo: A friend! what friend? your name, I pray you,
    friend.
Stephano: Stephano is my name; and I bring word
    My mistress will before the break of day
    Be here at Belmont: she doth stray about   30
    By holy crosses, where she kneels and prays
    For happy wedlock hours.
Lorenzo: Who comes with her?
Stephano: None but a holy hermit and her maid.
    I pray you, is my master yet return'd?
Lorenzo: He is not, nor we have not heard from him.   35
    But go we in, I pray thee, Jessica,
    And ceremoniously let us prepare
    Some welcome for the mistress of the house.
    Enter Launcelot
Launcelot: Sola, sola! wo ha, ho! sola, sola!
Lorenzo: Who calls?   40
Launcelot: Sola! did you see Master Lorenzo? Master
    Lorenzo! sola, sola!
Lorenzo: Leave hollowing, man; here.
Launcelot: Sola! where? where?
Lorenzo: Here.   45
Launcelot: Tell him there's a post come from my master,
    with his horn full of good news: my master will be here
    ere morning.   [*Exit*]
Lorenzo: Sweet soul, let's in, and there expect their coming.
    And yet no matter; why should we go in?   50
    My friend Stephano, signify, I pray you,
    Within the house, your mistress is at hand;
    And bring your music forth into the air. [*Exit Stephano*]
    How sweet the moonlight sleeps upon this bank!
    Here will we sit, and let the sounds of music   55
    Creep in our ears: soft stillness and the night
    Become the touches of sweet harmony.
    Sit, Jessica—look how the floor of heaven
    Is thick inlaid with patens of bright gold:

60   *orb:* circle (that is, a star or planet)

61   *his motion:* its movement

62   *still quiring:* forever singing in perfect harmony; *young-eyed cherubins:* bright-eyed angels

60-65   *There's not . . . hear it:* The Elizabethans believed that, as the stars and the planets moved through the heavens, they created musical harmony. However, as Lorenzo explains, we cannot hear this music as long as the soul is trapped in the body.

64   *muddy vesture of decay:* clothing of mortality (that is, the body)

65   *grossly:* roughly, coarsely

66   *Diana:* the classical goddess of the moon. Each evening, she comes down from heaven to sleep with her mortal lover Endymion (line 109).

69   *I am never . . . sweet music:* Jessica notes that listening to music makes her solemn and philosophical.

71   *wanton:* frisky

72   *race:* small group; *unhandled:* unbroken

73   *Fetching mad bounds:* leaping about wildly

74   *condition:* nature

75   *perchance:* perhaps

76   *air:* melody

77   *make a mutual stand:* all stand still together

78   *modest:* gentle, calm

79   *the poet:* The Latin poet Ovid told the story of Orpheus, whose music could draw lifeless objects to his side.

80   *feign:* imagine, create

81   *Since naught so stockish:* for (there is) nothing so dull or stupid

84   *concord:* harmony

85   *stratagems:* plots, acts of deceit, deceptions; *spoils:* destruction

87   *affections:* personality; *Erebus:* the personification of darkness in classical mythology (the son of Chaos and brother of Night)

88   *Mark:* pay attention to

91   *naughty:* wicked

94   *substitute:* deputy, viceroy

95-96   *his state Empties itself:* his glory immediately disappears

There's not the smallest orb which thou behold'st   60
But in his motion like an angel sings,
Still quiring to the young-eyes cherubins;
Such harmony is in immortal souls,
But whilst this muddy vesture of decay
Doth grossly close it in, we cannot hear it.   65
Enter Musicians
Come, ho! and wake Diana with a hymn:
With sweetness touches pierce your mistress' ear,
And draw her home with music.   [*Music*]
Jessica: I am never merry when I hear sweet music.
Lorenzo: The reason is, your spirits are attentive: 70
For do but note a wild and wanton herd,
Or race of youthful and unhandled colts,
Fetching mad bounds, bellowing and neighing loud,
Which is the hot condition of their blood;
If they but hear perchance a trumpet sound,   75
Or any air of music touch their ears,
You shall perceive them make a mutual stand,
Their savage eyes turn'd to a modest gaze
By the sweet power of music: therefore the poet
Did feign that Orpheus drew trees, stones, and floods;   80
Since naught so stockish, hard, and full of rage,
But music for the time doth change his nature.
The man that hath no music in himself,
Nor is not mov'd with concord of sweet sounds,
Is fit for treasons, stratagems, and spoils;   85
The motions of his spirit are dull as night,
And his affections dark as Erebus:
Let no such man be trusted. Mark the music.
Enter Portia and Nerissa
Portia: That light we see is burning in my hall.
How far that little candle throws his beams!   90
So shines a good deed in a naughty world.
Nerissa: When the moon shone, we did not see the candle.
Portia: So doth the greater glory dim the less:
A substitute shines brightly as a king
Until a king be by, and then his state   95
Empties itself, as doth an inland brook
Into the main of waters, Music! hark!

98   *your music . . . of the house:* As we saw in Act 3, Portia employs a small band of musicians as part of her household staff.

99   *Nothing . . . without respect:* Our judgments vary according to circumstances

103   *When neither is attended:* when each is alone.

104   *The nightingale . . . by day:* The nightingale was thought to sing only at night (when all other songbirds were asleep and silent).

107   *season:* good timing; *season'd:* improved

108   *right praise:* true value

115   *Which speed . . . the better for:* who benefit because of

119-120 *take No note:* say nothing

123   *tell-tales:* tellers of secrets

127   *Antipodes:* those people who live on the other side of the world

127-128 *We should hold . . . of the sun:* Bassanio's compliment corresponds roughly to our modern-day folksong, "You Are My Sunshine."

129   *light:* flighty, unfaithful

130   *heavy:* sad

Nerissa: It is your music, madam, of the house.
Portia: Nothing is good, I see, without respect:
   Methinks it sounds much sweeter than by day.   100
Nerissa: Silence bestows that virtue on it, madam.
Portia: The crow doth sing as sweetly as the lark
   When neither is attended, and I think
   The nightingale, if she should sing by day
   When every goose is cackling, would be thought   105
   No better a musician than the wren.
   How many things by season season'd are
   To their right praise and true perfection!
   Peace, ho! the moon sleeps with Endymion,
   And would not be awak'd!   *[Music ceases]* 110
Lorenzo: That is the voice,
   Or I am much deceiv'd, of Portia.
Portia: He knows me, as the blind man knows the cuckoo,
   By the bad voice.
Lorenzo: Dear lady, welcome home.
Portia: We have been praying for our husbands' welfare,
   Which speed, we hope, the better for our words.   115
   Are they return'd?
Lorenzo: Madam, they are not yet;
   But there is come a messenger before,
   To signify their coming.
Portia: Go in, Nerissa:
   Give order to my servants that they take
   No note at all of our being absent hence;   120
   Nor you, Lorenzo; Jessica, nor you.
                 [A trumpet sounds]
Lorenzo: Your husband is at hand, I hear his trumpet;
   We are no tell-tales, madam, fear you not.
Portia: This night methinks is but the daylight sick;
   It looks a little paler: 'tis a day,   125
   Such as the day is when the sun is hid.
   Enter Bassanio, Antonio, Gratiano, and their Servants
Bassanio: We should hold day with the Antipodes,
   If you would walk in absence of the sun.
Portia: Let me give light, but let me not be light;
   For a light wife doth make a heavy husband,   130
   And never be Bassanio so for me:

132   *God sort all:* let God make all the decisions

135   *bound:* indebted

138   *acquitted of:* released from

141   *scant:* cut short; *breathing courtesy:* polite conversation ("small talk")

144   *Would he were gelt:* I wish he had been castrated; *for my part:* as far as I'm concerned

145   *at heart:* to heart

147   *paltry:* worthless

148   *posy:* sentimental phrase or verse engraved on a ring

149   *cutler's poetry:* Cutlers, or knife-makers, sometimes inscribed short verses on their knives.

151   *What:* why?

156   *respective:* careful

158   *on's:* on his

159   *and if:* if ever

162   *scrubbed:* stunted, short

164   *prating:* chattering

But God sort all! You are welcome home, my lord.
Bassanio: I thank you, madam. Give welcome to my friend:
    This is the man, this is Antonio,
    To whom I am so infinitely bound.   135
Portia: You should in all sense be much bound to him,
    For, as I hear, he was much bound for you.
Antonio: No more than I am well acquitted of.
Portia: Sir, you are very welcome to our house:
    It must appear in other ways than words,   140
    Therefore I scant this breathing courtesy.
Gratiano: [*To Nerissa*] By yonder moon I swear you do me
      wrong;
    In faith, I give it to the judge's clerk;
    Would he were gelt that had it, for my part,
    Since you do take it, love, so much at heart.   145
Portia: A quarrel, ho, already! what's the matter?
Gratiano: About a hoop of gold, a paltry ring
    That she did give me, whose posy was
    For all the world like cutler's poetry
    Upon a knife, 'Love me, and leave me not'.   150
Nerissa: What talk you of the posy, or the value?
    You swore to me, when I did give it you,
    That you would wear it till your hour of death,
    And that it should lie with you in your grave:
    Though not for me, yet for your vehement oaths,   155
    You should have been respective and have kept it.
    Gave it a judge's clerk! no, God's my judge,
    The clerk will ne'er wear hair on's face that had it.
Gratiano: He will, and if he live to be a man.
Nerissa: Ay, if a woman live to be a man.   160
Gratiano: Now, by this hand, I gave it to a youth,
    A kind of boy, a little scrubbed boy,
    No higher than thyself, the judge's clerk.
    A prating boy that begg'd it as a fee:
    I could not for my heart deny it him.   165
Portia: You were to blame—I must be plain with you—
    To part so slightly with your wife's first gift;
    A thing stuck on with oaths upon your finger,
    And so riveted with faith unto your flesh.
    I gave my love a ring and made him swear   170

172 *leave:* part with

174 *masters:* possesses

176 *And 'twere to me:* if it had been done to me

198 *abate:* lessen

199 *virtue:* power

201 *contain:* keep, look after

205 *terms of zeal:* determination

205-206 *wanted the modesty . . . ceremony:* that he could have been so bad-mannered as to insist on having something that was so important to you

Never to part with it: and here he stands;
I dare be sworn for him he would not leave it,
Not pluck it from his finger, for the wealth
That the world masters. Now, in faith, Gratiano,
You give your wife too unkind a cause of grief: 175
And 'twere to me, I should be mad at it.
Bassanio: [*Aside*] Why, I were best to cut my left hand off,
And swear I lost the ring defending it.
Gratiano: My Lord Bassanio gave his ring away
Unto the judge that begg'd it, and indeed 180
Deserv'd it too; and then the boy, his clerk,
That took some pains in writing, he begg'd mine;
And neither man nor master would take aught
But the two rings.
Portia: What ring gave you, my lord?
Not that, I hope, which you receiv'd of me. 185
Bassanio: If I could add a lie unto a fault,
I would deny it; but you see my finger
Hath not the ring upon it—it is gone.
Portia: Even so void is your false heart of truth.
By heaven, I will ne're come in your bed 190
Until I see the ring.
Nerissa: Nor I in yours,
Till I again see mine.
Bassanio: Sweet Portia,
If you did know to whom I gave the ring,
If you did know for whom I gave the ring,
And would conceive for what I gave the ring, 195
And how unwillingly I left the ring,
When naught would be accepted but the ring,
You would abate the strength of your displeasure.
Portia: If you had known the virtue of the ring,
Or half her worthiness that gave the ring, 200
Or your own honour to contain the ring,
You would not then have parted with the ring.
What man is there so much unreasonable,
If you had pleas'd to have defended it
With any terms of zeal, wanted the modesty 205
To urge the thing held as a ceremony?
Nerissa teaches me what to believe:

208 *I'll die for 't:* I'm sure. Notice how Portia's mock anger moves her to hyperbole.

210 *civil doctor:* both a doctor of *civil law* and a *well-bred* doctor

213 *suffer'd:* allowed

214 *held up:* saved (that is, argued for)

217 *beset:* overcome

219 *besmear:* stain (my honour)

220 *blessed candles of the night:* the stars

226 *liberal:* free in giving

229 *know:* Shakespeare's audience would interpret this verb in a sexual sense.

230 *Argus:* in classical mythology, a creature with a hundred eyes. Juno hired him to keep jealous watch over one of her unfaithful husband's lovers.

234 *be well advis'd:* be careful

235 *to mine own protection:* to guard my own honour

236 *take:* catch

237 *mar:* damage

239 *notwithstanding:* nonetheless

240 *this enforced wrong:* this crime which was forced upon me

I'll die for 't, but some woman had the ring.
Bassanio: No, by my honour, madam, by my soul,
    No woman had it, but a civil doctor,   210
    Which did refuse three thousand ducats of me,
    And begg'd the ring, the which I did deny him,
    And suffer'd him to go displeas'd away;
    Even he that had held up the very life
    Of my dear friend. What should I say, sweet lady?   215
    I was enforc'd to send it after him.
    I was beset with shame and courtesy;
    My honour would not let ingratitude
    So much besmear it. Pardon me, good lady,
    For by these blessed candles of the night,   220
    Had you been there, I think you would have begg'd
    The ring of me to give the worthy doctor.
Portia: Let not that doctor e'er come near my house.
    Since he hath got the jewel that I lov'd,
    And that which you did swear to keep for me;   225
    I will become as liberal as you—
    I'll not deny him anything I have,
    No, not my body, nor my husband's bed.
    Know him I shall, I am well sure of it.
    Lie not a night from home; watch me like Argus: 230
    If you do not, if I be left alone,
    Now by mine honour, which is yet mine own,
    I'll have that doctor for my bedfellow.
Nerissa: And I his clerk; therefore be well advis'd
    How you do leave me to mine own protection.   235
Gratiano: Well, do you so: let not me take him, then,
    For if I do, I'll mar the young clerk's pen.
Antonio: I am th' unhappy subject of these quarrels.
Portia: Sir, grieve not you; you are welcome notwith-
    standing.
Bassanio: Portia, forgive me this enforced wrong;   240
    And in the hearing of these many friends,
    I swear to thee, even by thine own fair eyes,
    Wherein I see myself—
Portia: Mark you but that!
    In both my eyes he doubly sees himself;
    In each eye, one: swear by your double self,   245

246   *oath of credit:* believable promise (not believable, of course, at all if Portia's *double* means deceitful)

249   *wealth:* well-being, welfare

251   *had . . . miscarried:* would have been lost

253   *advisedly:* deliberately

254   *surety:* guarantee

262   *In lieu of:* in return for

263-264 *this is like . . . fair enough:* A new wife should not need a lover when her young husband is still lusty and amorous. Her taking of a lover is like repairing roads in summer – completely unnecessary.

265   *cuckolds:* men whose wives are unfaithful

266   *grossly:* indecently, coarsely; *amaz'd:* confused, befuddled

277   *are richly come:* have arrived with rich cargo; *suddenly:* unexpectedly

279   *dumb:* speechless

And there's an oath of credit.
Bassanio: Nay, but hear me:
    Pardon this fault, and by my soul I swear
    I never more will break an oath with thee.
Antonio: I once did lend my body for his wealth,
    Which, but for him that had your husband's ring,   250
    Had quite miscarried: I dare be bound again,
    My soul upon the forfeit, that your lord
    Will never more break faith advisedly.
Portia: Then you shall be his surety. Give him this,
    And bid him keep it better than the other.   255
Antonio: Here, Lord Bassanio; swear to keep this ring.
Bassanio: By heaven! it is the same I gave the doctor!
Portia: I had it of him: pardon me, Bassanio,
    For, by this ring, the doctor lay with me.
Nerissa: And pardon me, my gentle Gratiano;   260
    For that same scrubbed boy, the doctor's clerk,
    In lieu of this, last night did lie with me.
Gratiano: Why, this is like the mending of highways
    In summer, where the ways are fair enough!
    What, are we cuckolds ere we have deserv'd it?   265
Portia: Speak not so grossly. You are all amaz'd:
    Here is a letter, read it at your leisure,
    It comes from Padua, from Bellario:
    There you shall find that Portia was the doctor,
    Nerissa there her clerk. Lorenzo here   270
    Shall witness I set forth as soon as you,
    And even but now return'd; I have not yet
    Enter'd my house. Antonio, you are welcome;
    And I have better news in store for you
    Than you expect: unseal this letter soon;   275
    There you shall find three of your argosies
    Are richly come to harbour suddenly.
    You shall not know by what strange accident
    I chanced on this letter.
Antonio: I am dumb.
Bassanio: Were you the doctor, and I knew you not?   280
Gratiano: Were you the clerk that is to make me cuckold?
Nerissa: Ay, but the clerk that never means to do it,
    Unless he live until he be a man.

288   *road:* anchorage (see note on Act 1, Scene 1, line 19)

294   *manna:* the miraculous food which fell from the sky for the Israelites as they were starving in the wilderness on their journey from Egypt to the promised land (*Exodus* 16:15) Lorenzo uses the allusion to mean unexpected fortune.

297   *at full:* in detail

298   *charge us . . . inter'gatories:* In court, witnesses were called upon to answer under oath a series of questions (*interrogatories*).

305   *That:* so that; *couching:* going to bed (from the French, *coucher*)

307   *sore:* sorely, greatly, highly

Bassanio: Sweet doctor, you shall be my bedfellow:
    When I am absent, then lie with my wife. 285
Antonio: Sweet lady, you have given me life and living;
    For here I read for certain that my ships
    Are safely come to road.
Portia: How now, Lorenzo!
    My clerk hath some good comforts too for you.
Nerissa: Ay, and I'll give them him without a fee. 290
    There do I give to you and Jessica,
    From the rich Jew, a special deed of gift,
    After his death, of all he dies possess'd of.
Lorenzo: Fair ladies, you drop manna in the way
    Of starved people. 295
Portia: It is almost morning,
    And yet I am sure you are not satisfied
    Of these events at full. Let us go in;
    And charge us there upon inter'gatories,
    And we will answer all things faithfully.
Gratiano: Let it be so: the first inter'gatory 300
    That my Nerissa shall be sworn on is,
    Whether till the next night she had rather stay,
    Or go to bed now, being two hours to day:
    But were the day come, I should wish it dark,
    That I were couching with the doctor's clerk. 305
    Well, while I live, I'll fear no other thing
    So sore as keeping safe Nerissa's ring.   [*Exeunt*]

Act 5, Scene 1: Activities

1. This scene begins with a spirited contest in which Lorenzo and Jessica compete to "out-night" each other with a series of allusions to famous lovers in classical literature.

   Make a list of other pairs of lovers whose stories they might have used in their competition. For the story of each pair, identify the event which best suggests the romantic atmosphere of the night-time setting in Lorenzo and Jessica's stories. You may need to embellish some of the stories with original incidents and details to achieve this. Be sure to include a variety of mythological, historical, and contemporary pairs. Romeo and Juliet, Orpheus and Eurydice, Samson and Delilah, Frankie and Johnny, Antony and Cleopatra, and the Duke and Duchess of Windsor are some examples.

   Try extending the out-nighting dialogue between Lorenzo and Jessica, using your best examples. If you enjoy the challenge of writing verse, try to follow the metrical pattern established in the dialogue.

2. Assume you are the musical director of a production of *The Merchant of Venice* and you have to choose music to accompany lines 54-110 of this scene. What music would you choose? With a partner, select a portion of these lines to read to the class with the music you have chosen in the background. With the class, discuss how appropriate and effective your choice of music is.

3. Much of the humour in the dialogue about the rings comes not from the lines alone, but from the looks, the gestures, and the vocal inflections that would be used by the actors.

   In groups of four or five, experiment with lines 142 to 193. Discuss fully the ways in which you could maximize the humour in playing the scene. Rehearse and present your version to the class.

4. Shakespeare does not explain how Antonio's ships have been saved or why they were missing for so long. Imagine that the letter Portia delivers is from Antonio's business manager in Venice. Write the letter, explaining why there has been such a serious misunderstanding, and how Antonio's three ships were saved.

5. a) The play ends on a note of harmony and celebration as Antonio and the three loving couples laugh and joke together. Do you think Shakespeare expects the audience to believe that the characters will all live "happily ever after," as in a fairy tale? Discuss your ideas with others.

   b) Assume that, as Shakespeare, you want to write a sequel to this play, set five years later. Prepare brief notes to describe the circumstances of the main characters at the start of your new play. How have their lives changed now that the celebrations of *The Merchant of Venice* have faded into memory? For instance, has Bassanio wasted all of Portia's wealth? Has Antonio succeeded in business, or has he suffered through more risky business ventures? How have Nerissa and Gratiano settled into married life? How are Jessica and Lorenzo supporting themselves until they can inherit Shylock's money? How has Shylock adapted to life as a Christian? Have he and Jessica been reconciled?

   Summarize your notes and compare them with summaries prepared by classmates.

Consider the Whole Play

1. Now that you have finished your reading of *The Merchant of Venice*, you will probably want to discuss, in small groups or as a class, some of the issues and concerns upon which the play is built. Some of the main questions include:
   - What are the values and responsibilities of friendship?
   - What is "true love"?
   - Why are we so often "deceived with ornament"?
   - What are the obligations of children to parents, and parents to children?
   - When is a risk worth taking?
   - Can there be justice without mercy?
   - Are there rules or laws which *should* be broken?

   In your discussion, consider how your understanding of the play and your personal experience lead you to your conclusions.

   Write about one of these topics in your journal. Answer the question with examples from your own experience or use examples taken from events in the play.

2. *The Merchant of Venice* is a play about which there are many opposing views. Consider all of the following topics and choose one for formal classroom debate. Prepare your argument and be ready to defend it in the context of your knowledge of the whole play.

   a) Shylock's famous speech, "Hath not a Jew eyes?" is a cold-blooded justification of revenge, not a plea for tolerance.

   b) The world is still deceived with ornament.

   c) Bassanio is a superficial fool.

   d) Money is more important than friendship.

   e) Obedience to parents is a child's prime obligation.

   f) Nothing can be gained without risk.

g) It is impossible for a modern audience to enjoy *The Merchant of Venice* because of the play's prejudice.

3. Many teenagers identify with Shylock's predicament more easily than adults and, consequently, share a common bond with him. Perhaps the fact that many teens feel themselves to be persecuted or "outsiders" provides one explanation for this attachment.

   In small groups, discuss the validity of this observation. Consider carefully your own reaction to Shylock and his predicament and the reactions of your classmates. Do you identify at all with Shylock? Do you think that your situation resembles his in any way?

   Organize your own thoughts and feelings in a personal essay, or use your ideas as the basis for a short story or poem about a contemporary teen in a similar situation.

4. As a class, publish a newspaper that might appear in Venice on the day after the trial. You will need to divide yourselves into "sections": world news, local news, editorial page, sports, "society" page, want ads, and others you may choose, with section editors reporting to the editor-in-chief.

   Section editors should assign stories to each group member. Stories may be researched and written independently or in pairs. Reporters submit copy to their section editors for proofreading; revised copy is then submitted to the editor-in-chief for consideration.

   A meeting of all editors will be needed to make final editorial decisions and to determine the layout of the paper.

   You might need assistance in having the paper duplicated; perhaps you could arrange to have copies made at a print shop.

   Have fun!

5. A knowledge of the importance of Venice during the Renaissance greatly enhances our appreciation of the society presented in *The Merchant of Venice*.

Find out all you can about Medieval Venice. In your research you might consider some of the following topics:
   - the advantages of Venice's geographical position
   - the goods most often traded in Venice
   - the cosmopolitan character of the city
   - the architectural and artistic splendour of the city
   - the establishment of banks
   - the way the city was governed

Two books you might find helpful are:
McNeill, W.H., *Venice: The Hinge of Europe*
Morris, Jan, *The Venetian Empire: A Sea Voyage*

Create a *presentation* which will involve your classmates in the experience of Venice. Take full advantage of the wealth of visual material available (slides, postcards, maps, travel brochures) and use your imagination to bring Venice to your classroom.

6. Portia, Nerissa, and Jessica all appear in *The Merchant of Venice* disguised as young men. *Twelfth Night* and *As You Like It* are two other Shakespearean comedies which have heroines in male disguise. Many other works of fiction also have included female heroines disguised as males.

With the help of your teacher or librarian, locate and read one of these works to discover the reason for the disguise, the troubles and conflicts the disguise causes, and the contribution it makes to the final out-come. Present your findings to the class.

7. What is the difference between a comedy and a tragedy?

   a) In your notebook, outline the differences between comedy and tragedy. Which would you call *The Merchant of Venice*? Does your answer hold true for all the characters?

b) Consider the four sub-plots of the play: the bond plot, the casket plot, the ring plot and the elopement plot. Identify the point in each plot at which you became sure it would have a happy ending.

c) In a small group, choose one plot and reinvent its outcome. How would the events of the other two plots have to change as a result? Present an outline of your revised plot to the class, explaining how one change would affect the events of the whole play.

8. *The Merchant of Venice* contains many lines and images which stimulate creative thought. Use one of the following quotations as a springboard for creative writing. Before you begin, decide on a purpose for writing and on an intended audience. Consider writing a short story, a fable or myth, a personal essay, a newspaper editorial, poetry, a dialogue, a short playscript, or a letter. In reality, you are limited only by the power of your imagination!

a) The world is still deceived with ornament.

b) I never knew so young a body with so old a head.

c) So shines a good deed in a naughty world.

d) O me, the word "choose"!

e) He finds the joys of heaven here on earth.

f) All things that are,
Are with more spirit chased than enjoy'd.

g) I have much ado to know myself.

h) Alack, what heinous sin is it in me
To be asham'd to be my father's child!

i) O what a goodly outside falsehood hath!

j) It is a wise father that knows his own child.

k) The man that hath no music in himself . . .
Let no such man be trusted.

Be sure to "publish" your work, sharing it with other members of the class and contributing it to your school or community paper or magazine.

9. Shakespeare's plays, like all Renaissance literature, abound in allusions or references to mythology and the Bible. These allusions reflect the fascination of the time with knowledge, both of the sciences and the arts. Elizabethans considered Greek and Roman literature and the Bible to represent the accumulated wisdom of the ancient world.

   Complete a list of five of the classical and Biblical allusions in *The Merchant of Venice*. Examine each of these allusions to determine its purpose, particularly in terms of Shakespeare's development of his characters and themes. Use this information to prepare a presentation to the class on the contribution of allusions to this play.

10. Stereotypes need not be religious, national, or cultural, We live each day surrounded by more common stereotypes: the misunderstood teenager, the right-wing bigot, the bleeding-heart liberal, the ineffectual parent, the befuddled teacher. These stereotypes abound on television and radio and in films, comic strips, and music videos.

    In a small group, collect as many examples of media stereotyping as you can. Sort and label your evidence in order to arrive at categories which classify the kinds of stereotyping that you found. Sort your evidence *again* according to the intentions and purposes the examples seem to serve. A *third* sorting might measure the degree of harm or danger you find in each example.

    Report the group's conclusions to the class. Allow full time for discussion and response.

11. The Passover prayer book, *The Haggadah*, contains the following statement:
    "In every generation, someone rises up against us, to annihilate us."

    Starting with a good encyclopedia, survey the history of anti-Semitic persecution in Europe and North America. Select a single example and research it in detail. Focus on the causes and repercussions of the persecution rather than the accumulation of statistics and details. Share your discoveries and observations with your group and prepare a presentation to the class. Allow time for full discussion and response.

    Two books you might find helpful are the following: *The Anguish of the Jews*, Edward H. Flannery and *A History of the Jews*, Paul Johnson.

12. Read one of the following twentieth century novels, biographies, and autobiographies as a companion piece to *The Merchant of Venice*. In all of these works, the issue of racial or cultural prejudice is important. Prepare a "book talk" for your group or class, in which you review the book and comment upon its similarities and parallels with *The Merchant of Venice*. Consider especially the causes and effects of prejudice in the book.

    Biographies

    Bennet, Levone: *What Manner of Man* (Martin Luther King, Jr.)
    Broadfoot, Barry: *Years of Sorrow, Years of Shame*
    Frank, Anne: *Diary of a Young Girl*
    Griffin, John H: *Black Like Me*
    Kuper, Jack: *Child of the Holocaust*
    Kwinta, Chava: *I'm Still Living*
    Malcolm X and Haley, Alex: *The Autobiography of Malcolm X*
    Meir, Golda: *My Life*
    Suzuki, David: *Metamorphosis*

Fiction

Achebe, Chinua: *Things Fall Apart*
Ball, John: *In the Heat of the Night*
Bonham, Frank: *Chief*
Cameron, Anne: *Daughters of Copper Woman*
Campbell,Maria: *Half-breed*
Craven, Margaret: *I Heard the Owl Call My Name*
Greene, Betty: *Summer of My German Soldier*
Greene, Hannah: *I Never Promised You a Rose Garden*
Haley, Alex: *Roots*
Hinton, S.E.: *The Outsiders*
Kogawa, Joy: *Obasan*
Keyes, Daniel: *Flowers for Algernon*
Lee, Harper: *To Kill a Mockingbird*
Malamud, Bernard: *The Fixer*
Markandaya, Kamale: *The Nowhere Man*
Marlyn, John: *Under the Ribs of Death*
Marshall, James Vance: *Walkabout*
Richter, Hans P.: *Friedrich*
Samuels, Gertrude: *Mottele*
Steinbeck, John: *Of Mice and Men*
Such, Peter: *Riverrun*
Ten Boom, Corrie: *The Hiding Place*
Walker, Alice: *The Color Purple*
Wiesel, Elie: *Night*
Wright, Richard: *Native Son*

Your teacher or librarian could discuss these and other books with you and assist you in making a selection.

13. Is Shylock a "good" Jew? Does he display any of the qualities, attitudes, or beliefs that the Jewish faith holds dear? Research this question, starting with a good encyclopedia before moving to one of these books on Judaism:
   Hertzberg, Arthur, ed: *Judaism* (in the series *Great Religions of Modern Man*)
   Rosenberg, Stuart: *To Understand Jews.*
   Wouk, Herman: *This is my God: The Jewish Way of Life.*

An interview with a rabbi or Jewish community leader would also be very useful.

When you have a grasp of what Judaism teaches, return to the play and examine Shylock's behaviour to determine whether he may accurately be called a "a good Jew."

Your findings and conclusions could take the form of an essay or a class report.

A parallel project could examine the extent to which Antonio (or Bassanio, Portia, or Gratiano) can be called "a good Christian."

14. Many schools and school boards have decided that *The Merchant of Venice* is an unsuitable play for classroom study, on the grounds that it may be offensive to some students.

   From your study of the play, list the reasons you think some people are offended by it. What is your own response to each of these objections? Do you consider them sufficient grounds for removing the play from the curriculum?

   In a small group, discuss these issues fully, giving careful and thoughtful consideration to the point of view of every member of the group. Organize and record the conclusions you reach in a personal essay, position paper, or short speech.

15. Twentieth century responses to *The Merchant of Venice* seem to suggest that modern society has become more concerned about the rights and freedoms of individuals and minority groups. Many events and movements have contributed to our growing understanding and tolerance of others:

   (a) the suffragettes

   (b) the holocaust

   (c) the creation of the United Nations

(d) the American civil rights movement

(e) women's liberation

(f) anti-apartheid protests

(g) Third World refugees

(h) Amnesty International

Investigate one of these (or another important example of which you are aware). Discover the causes, the issues, and the results or repercussions of the example you choose. Concentrate on the ways it has changed our attitudes towards others.

Present your observations and conclusions in an essay or class report.